NATURE AND TECHNOLOGY IN THE WORLD RELIGIONS

NATURE AND TECHNOLOGY IN THE WORLD RELIGIONS

Edited by

PETER KOSLOWSKI

Hannover Institute of Philosophical Research,
Hannover, Germany

KLUWER ACADEMIC PUBLISHERS
DORDRECHT / BOSTON / LONDON

A C.I.P. Catalogue record for this book is available from the Library of Congress.

ISBN 1-4020-0188-6 (HB)
ISBN 1-4020-0055-3 (Set)

Published by Kluwer Academic Publishers,
P.O. Box 17, 3300 AA Dordrecht, The Netherlands.

Sold and distributed in North, Central and South America
by Kluwer Academic Publishers,
101 Philip Drive, Norwell, MA 02061, U.S.A.

In all other countries, sold and distributed
by Kluwer Academic Publishers,
P.O. Box 322, 3300 AH Dordrecht, The Netherlands.

Printed with the Support of the Foundation of Lower Saxony
(Stiftung Niedersachsen)

The German language version of this book is published simultaneously by
WILHELM FINK VERLAG
Munich

Editorial Assistant: David W. Lutz

Cover Photograph:
JANNIS KOUNELLIS, Untitled, 1967
Gerald Zugmann / MAK – Österreichisches Museum für Angewandte Kunst, Wien

Printed on acid-free paper

TABLE OF CONTENTS

FOREWORD

Modern technology brings about an enlargement of human power, which causes the religious idea of the subordination of human beings to the power of God and the order of being or of nature to appear obsolete. Technology makes possible the greater development, strengthening, and expansion of human organs by machines, going as far as replacing human intelligence by artificial intelligence, and thus brings about an enormous increase in the power of human persons. Humans create machines whose ability to perform exceeds that of humans. Why should anyone, in view of such works of the technological world, acknowledge the normativeness of nature and of the religious order of being? On the other hand, man is overcome by fear of his own products, because he is also always subject to them, and it appears to him that self-subjugation to a divine law might provide and protect freedom better than the self-subjugation of humans to their own technological products.

Has the religious relationship of the veneration of nature been superseded? Are we free not only, as religions assume, to further creation by technology, but also to surpass it? Or does the normativeness of nature gain in importance when the technological control of human nature and of natural nature increases, because the questions of what the telos of intervention in nature is and where the boundaries of the transformability of nature lie become all the more threatening? What descriptions and solutions of problems related to the question of the self-increase or the self-loss of the human person through technology have the world religions worked out? Where are the differences and the points of agreement in the relationship to nature between the Abrahamic religions, Christianity, Judaism, and Islam, which regard nature as creation, and Hinduism and Buddhism, in which the idea of creation does not stand at the center in the same way?

This third volume in the series A Discourse of the World Religions takes up the question of the relationship to nature and the interpretation of technology in the world religions, which was posed by the topic of the World Exposition EXPO 2000 Hanover, "Humankind, Nature, Technology." It applies the question to the world religions and seeks to answer it from their perspectives. The book documents the Third EXPO-Discourse, which took place on 22-23 June 2000, at the beginning of the World Exposition EXPO 2000 in Hanover, Germany. The theme of the conference was "Humankind's Relationship with Nature and Participation in the Process of Creation by Technology in the View of the World Religions." It was convened in the pavilion of the Norddeutsche Landesbank (NORD/LB) at the World Exposition in Hanover. The organizers of the conference were the Hanover Institute of Philosophical Research and the Foundation of Lower Saxony.

I would like to thank the Norddeutsche Landesbank Girozentrale for its hospitality to the conference in the NORD/LB Forum, its conference center at the grounds of the World Exposition, now the Hanover Exhibition Grounds, as well as for logistical help. I would also like to thank the Foundation of Lower Saxony and the Foundation of the Hanover Institute of Philosophical Research for making the entire project possible, as well as the members of the Hanover Institute of Philosophical Research for their support in preparing for and conducting the EXPO-Discourses.

Peter Koslowski

INTRODUCTION TO THE THREE DISCOURSES AT THE WORLD EXPOSITION EXPO 2000 HANOVER "HUMANKIND, NATURE, TECHNOLOGY"

Why is it meaningful to conduct a Discourse of the World Religions at the 2000 World Exposition in Hanover, Germany? The multiplicity of religions is an outrage for those who are not religious and a problem for those who are. The former see in this multiplicity only a source of never-ending conflicts, which lead to nothing but new conflicts. It appears to non-religious persons, therefore, that the enlightenment of the human race requires destroying the entire nightmare of religions. Religious persons, on the other hand, recognize a problem in the multiplicity of religions, an unnatural, forced situation that calls their own faith into question. How can God permit a state of the world in which there exist groups of people, each including hundreds of millions of members, which understand and invoke him by completely different names? How can the one God be venerated by people in completely different ways, when he is the Lord of the world and the Lord of history? It seems that, as the Lord of history, he should have hindered the development of a situation in which there could be as many different convictions about his name and his nature as the multiplicity and diversity of the world religions has produced.

Within the multiplicity of religions there exists a theodicy problem: How can the situation of the multiplicity of religions in the world be compatible with the conviction that God is omnipotent and morally perfect? Two theodicy questions for the theology of religion arise from the multiplicity of the world religions. Both the radically exclusive conviction that only one of the existing religions is true and the radically inclusive view that all religions represent merely traces of the truth raise the theodicy question of why God permits the multiplicity and diversity of religions in the world.

If one is convinced that there is only one true religion, that poses the question of how the omnipotent God can permit so many people to be ignorant of that fact and to belong to other, heterodox faiths. If, on the contrary, one is convinced that all religions are merely traces of the truth, one must explain why God does not reveal himself to humanity as himself, why he hides himself so much that none of the existing religions is his full revelation. One must then ascribe to him, as Severus of Antioch in antiquity and Hegel in the nineteenth century already have, jealousy and a will not to reveal himself.

Since the multiplicity of religions is outrageous for those who are not religious and vexing for those who are, both groups would gladly be rid of the multiplicity of religions in the world, the former by the abolition of religion entirely and the latter by superseding all other religions by their own or by separating the world religions according to world regions: Each religion would receive a corner of the world, and there would be as little exchange as possible between them.

A world exposition worthy of its name must by definition be the opposite of this latter solution. In order to represent the world as it is, it must portray the multiplicity of religions on its grounds. And if it is really to bring the people of the world together, it must bring together the world religions, because hardly anything shapes the character of the world's people, their interpretations of existence and the structure of their lives, as much as their religions. A world exposition that truly wishes to address what is on humanity's mind, cannot disregard the problem of the multiplicity of the great religions. It can exclude this question in the face of neither the critics nor the friends of religion. It must make its contribution toward defusing the conflicts among religions for secular people just as much as toward promoting genuine dialogue among religious people of different faiths.

A dialogue of the religions is also unavoidable for another reason. The globalization of our life-world no longer permits the solution that each religion may determine the character of its own region and be the mistress of the religious house there – the principle *cuius regio, eius religio* – according to which the coexistence of the different confessions was regulated in Germany after the Reformation. The present globalization goes beyond the internationalization of previous decades. We no longer live and produce as nations for the international market; we live in nations that are determined by more than a religious and cultural tradition, and we produce intellectually and economically within a global context with contributions from many regions of the world. Our economic and intellectual life is increasingly characterized not only by international, but also by global exchange, which necessarily leads to a global encounter of the religions. Supporting this global conversation of the religions of the world at the 2000 World Exposition in Hanover was the wish and the intention of the three EXPO Discourses at the World Exposition in the year 2000.

To expand this conversation beyond the personal meeting of persons at the World Exposition to a worldwide exchange between authors and readers is the wish and intention of this series A Discourse of the World Religions.

P. K.

NATURE AND TECHNOLOGY IN THE RELIGIONS

Peter Koslowski

The World Exposition EXPO 2000 in Hanover adopted as its theme the relationships of humanity to nature and technology. This suggested making "nature and technology" a central theme of the inter-religious and "inter-philosophical" dialogue of the project Discourse of the World Religions before and during the World Exposition. The reasons for the occasion of the World Exposition and the systematic reasons for the centrality of the theme coincided. For the relationship of humans to nature is a central object of religious doctrine and ethics in all world religions. Since the religions respond to the neediness of human life, they cannot ignore the cause of this neediness, the tense relationship between the needs of our lives and the scope of the means in nature at our disposal. They cannot avoid addressing the relationship of the human person to nature and to technology as a means of increasing the yield from nature.

Technology and the economy are, as Friedrich von Gottl-Ottlilienfeld has shown, a means of liberating human beings from their predicament, from the predicaments of external nature and the predicaments of social dependence.[1] Both aim at the productive resolution of the predicament and thus at order: "According to their idea, consequently, the economy is order in the actions of meeting needs and technology is order in the carrying out of these actions."[2] The order in the economy and the order in technology are part of the order of life and thus of the order of the religions and cannot possibly stand outside the life orders conceived and determined by the religions.

In addition to the practical, religiously-influenced, even if not religiously-determined relationship of the human race to nature in the economy and technology, there is also the relationship of humankind to nature that is religious in the narrower sense. Nature is venerated in the nature mysticism of the religions; it is elevated in cult and rite. The "Last Supper" and the Eucharist of Christianity are examples, as natural nourishment is elevated to the level of spiritual nourishment. Nature is seen in the religions as the mystery through which the higher world shines into the lower. For the world religions, the natural is the beginning

---

[1] Cf. Friedrich von Gottl-Ottlilienfeld, *Grundriß der Sozialökonomik, II. Abteilung: Die natürlichen und technischen Beziehungen der Wirtschaft, Teil 2: Wirtschaft und Technik*, 2nd Rev. Ed. (Tübingen: Mohr Siebeck, 1923; repr. Frankfurt: Keip, 1985), p. 10.
[2] Ibid.

P. Koslowski (eds), Nature and Technology in the World Religions, 1–17.
© 2001 *Kluwer Academic Publishers. Printed in the Netherlands.*

of the supernatural – not a beginning that can simply be left behind idealistically in the ascent to spirituality, but one that also has normative meaning in this life. Thus the importance of the body in all religions, in the Western tradition in Judaism and Christianity, but also in the Eastern traditions of Hinduism and Buddhism, as well as in Islam, which stands between East and West. The natural can be seen as a bridge to the spiritual in the significance of the garden and of bodily concentration exercises in Buddhism.

Paradoxically, the world religions, which attach special significance to eternal life or life after death, also place great value upon careful treatment of the physical nature of human persons and the natural environment that surrounds them in the life before death, whereas the secular Western world, which denies life after death, attaches less importance to the normativeness of traditional nature and subjects it to being completely at the disposal of human beings and their technology. This development is consistent with Max Weber's thesis that the end of nature mysticism and the veneration of nature, brought about by Protestantism, has brought about the modern domination of nature through technology.

1. Technology as Compensation for the Human Person as a Needy Creature and as Reform of Nature in the Religions

1.1. THE CONTINGENCY OF THE CREATION IN JUDAISM, CHRISTIANITY, AND ISLAM: GOD AS THE MAKER OF NATURE AND HUMANS AS HIS CO-WORKERS

For Judaism, Christianity, and Islam, the dialectic of availability and reverence of nature is characteristic. Nature is, on one hand, given to human rule by the commission to rule over nature in the biblical creation account,[3] and it is at the same time withdrawn from humans and not given over completely to their disposal, because it is the creation of a personal being, of the personal God. The human person must instead respect the prerogative of the true creator and owner of nature, according to the religious world view, and prove to be a vassal, a trustee and caretaker in the stewardship of nature. In addition, there is a second idea, which likewise leads to the characteristic dialectic of veneration of nature and distance from nature in Judaism and Christianity: the idea of the difference *and* connectedness of the creator and the creation, the author and the work, which is characteristic of the theological idea of creation. The Jewish, Christian, and also Islamic doctrines of creation are essential poietic and thereby technomorphic.

---

[3] Cf. the contributions by Micha Brumlik and Asghar Ali Engineer to this volume.

Even if the creation contains a technomorphic element through God, this does not imply that God is a technician. God cannot be a technician, because there is no universal technology of the creation of worlds. Because there is no technology of creation, God is not given any technology that existed before him or that he himself created. Since God created only one time, he needs no technology and also creates no technology of creation, because one does not create technology for a creative occurrence that occurs only one time: there is no technology for a singular event.[4]

According to Judaism, Christianity, and Islam, God makes the creation and he is the artist who both realizes himself in his work and is different from it in his substance and is not dependent upon it. He does not realize himself in his nature through his work, as Hegelianism and pantheism assume. The relationship of God and the world, creator and creation, is a relationship of subject and object, but neither a relationship of separation[5] nor one of the identity of subject and object, in which the subject God would be increasingly identical with his object, the world, as the identity-philosophers Hegel and Schelling assume.

The distinction, but not separation, of creator and creation anticipates the distinction of human producer and product, of the subjectivity of the human person and the objectivity of that which is produced, which is characteristic of every act of technological production. The producer does not first become conscious of himself and his spirit through his work on the object, as the elevation of the subject-object relationship in Hegel's logic assumes, but is instead already previously conscious and can create only because he is already conscious.[6]

The poietic analogy or analogy of poiesis, which considers the creation of nature to be something made and produced by a person, leads to a distancing of the human person from nature, because it is interpreted as a produced object and as a work that could also not exist, if its creator had chosen not to produce it. The idea of nature as creation means that nature possesses the mark of the contingent, of the non-necessary and non-eternal. Nature as creation is non-necessary and non-eternal, because it is not rooted in necessity, but in the freedom of the creative will of God, and it is not eternal and beginningless, but has its beginning in the six-day work of God, the *opus six dierum*, even if it is also created for eternity as the creation of God. The contingency of the creation in the will of the creator relativizes the holiness of nature in Judaism and Christianity: Nature could also not exist.

---

[4] Cf. D. P. Chattopadhyaya in this volume, p. 91.

[5] Cf. below Francis X. D'Sa, who brings out that the world is not an external object for God as its Creator.

[6] On the theory of creation, see Peter Koslowski, *Philosophien der Offenbarung: Antiker Gnostizismus, Franz von Baader, Schelling* (Paderborn: Schöningh, 2001), pp. 329-52 and 772-86.

The contingency of the creation is strengthened by its original state of being created for human beings. Already before the fall, nature is completed only by the collaboration of the human person in God's work of creation: God brought, as the creation account of Genesis 2,19 reads "every beast of the field and every bird of the heavens" to the man, so that he could name them: "And whatever the man called a living creature, that was its name." With this sentence in the Yah-wist creation account, the central, original collaboration of the human in the creation is expressed, which Judaism, Christianity, and also Islam accept already before the fall. The three ideas, the separation of creation and creature, the idea that the human person was created in the image of God and, therefore, according to his purpose, as likewise a creative being, and the idea that the human person is to participate in the work of creation bring about the distinction of man and nature and the dominant position of the human person relative to nature. This dominant position is not directed against nature. It implies, however, power and rule over nature.

Power can in turn be either good or bad rule. It does not necessarily decay into exploitation. Power is in danger of corrupting, great power is in great danger of corrupting. This is also true of human power over nature. The human person was corrupted by his power over nature and did not comply with his dominant position, thus read the theosophical interpretations of the biblical fall. The human person did not fall because of haughtiness and arrogance, but because of malice and laziness. He wanted to be like nature and, therefore, not to comply with his position as ruler over nature.

The biblical religions advocate the dominant position of the human person and his rule over nature. The relationship to nature determined by them is, therefore, subject to the ambivalence of the rule of nature and the danger of the non-respect of nature – perhaps to a greater degree than the nature relationship of Hinduism and Buddhism, which do not recognize the idea of the distinction of creator and nature and the idea of the contingency of creation to the same extent. There are, to be sure, traditions of Hinduism that also include a doctrine of creation.

Why is the idea of the collaboration of man in the creation so central to Judaism and Christianity? Why does the creator grant his creature, humanity, so much collaboration in the creation already before the fall? Man cannot make the creation better than the Creator himself; and it also reads that God saw that what he had made was good. Thus, the original collaboration of man in the creation must belong to that which was good in it. One cannot say more about the reasons that may have induced the Creator to will the collaboration of the creature.

1.2. TECHNOLOGY AS CONSEQUENCE OF AND COMPENSATION FOR THE FALL IN JUDAISM AND CHRISTIANITY

The doctrine of the fall, which occurred because man did not comply with his position, further strengthens the element of the collaboration of human persons in the creation – both by the idea that nature was changed for the worse by the fall of man and by the idea that the human person became through the fall a creature of deficiencies, who must himself remedy the deficits that he brought about in the world and himself by the effort of work and technology, as well as by the collaborative help of God: The human person has damaged nature and must now improve it with God's and his own help. Thus, the fall and the origin of technology move closely together. Technology became the prosthesis of fallen man, and he seeks with its help to compensate the deficiencies that he has caused for himself and nature by his fall. The fall is the *felix culpa* of technology. It has produced the deficient being man and the deficits of nature, which man will now heal by technology itself. Technology becomes, therefore, a component of the realization of the common good of the human race and the welfare of the human individual.

One can say with Friedrich Dessauer that God as it were continues the creation by means of technology.[7] Technology stands at the service of the realization of the creation and "the idea of technology is the idea of service" according to Dessauer.[8] At the same time, technology receives a dimension of historicity through the idea that it is compensation for deficiencies that have entered into the creation: It is a consequence of an historical fall and it should contribute to the realization of the common good in history in the historicity that entered through the fall.

This emphasis on historicity, the emphasis on historical revelation and the related thesis that divine revelation completes itself despite and through the fall, original sin, and historicity, as well as through the progress of humanity and technology, distinguishes Judaism and Christianity, so it appears, from the other religion that also recognizes its origin in the Bible: Islam. In Islam the verbal revelation of Allah in the Quran is more important than the historical revelation of God in and through history. This difference between Judaism and Christianity, on one hand, and Islam, on the other, can perhaps also explain the different degrees of the realization of technology in Islam and in Judaism and Christianity. In the culture of the West shaped by Christianity and Judaism, technology is an historical force of the compensation of deficiency and an element of the realization of the common good.

---

[7] Friedrich Dessauer, *Philosophie der Technik: Das Problem der Realisierung* (Bonn: Cohen, 1927), p. 86. The 5th Edition is entitled *Streit um die Technik* (Frankfurt: Knecht, 1956).

[8] Ibid., pp. 131ff.

1.3. TYPES OF TECHNOLOGY

Technology contributes to the common good as "real technology" (*Realtechnik*) in the economy, as the individual technology of the efficient lifestyle and spiritual "technology," as social technology in social and political organizations as well as intellectual technology in the academic disciplines and in the methodology of thinking.[9] Gottl-Ottlilienfeld distinguishes 1. Individual technology as intervention into the psychological-corporal constitution of the acting person himself and mnemonic technology, the technology of self-control, etc., 2. Social technology, as soon as the intervening action applies to the other and shapes the relationship to the other in the technology of the fight, of the occupation, in rhetoric and pedagogy, and in the technology of ruling and behaviour. In addition, he distinguishes 3. Intellectual technology as intervention into an intellectual situation, for example all methodologies, the technology of calculating, of the intellectual game, etc., and finally 4. Real technology as the epitome of technology, which applies itself to the external world and includes "the clarified entirety of the process and aids of the nature-ruling action."[10] In this comprehensive sense of technology, "technology and action belong together in a way similar to the relation between logic and thought."[11]

Christoph Hubig distinguishes the technology of action or work, the technology of machines, and the technology of systems according to their connection to the action, freedom, and justification problem of technology. While the technology of the use of tools begins at the level of action and implies value-freedom, which is only later concretized by choosing the ends for the use of means and, therefore, implies the controllability of the means *and* ends, as well as of one's own abilities and finally the control of reality, the degree of freedom in the use of the technologies of machines and systems decreases in proportion to the increase in effectiveness. With the technology of machines, *only ends* can still be chosen; the means-ends relations are determined by the construction of the machines. The technology of machines is centered around the opening and the actualizing of potentialities. Finally, systems and the technology of systems determine the ends *and* means of the system-context and can only still be chosen or rejected as a whole. The technology of systems determines the condition of the potentialities of the use of tools and machines within a more broadly developed technological system of means-end relations of the control of comprehensive

---

[9] Cf. The Editors, "Technik," *Historisches Wörterbuch der Philosophie*, ed. Joachim Ritter† and Karlfried Gründer, Vol. 10 (Basel: Schwabe, 1998), Cols. 940-52.

[10] On this distinction of forms of technology, cf. Gottl-Ottlilienfeld, p. 9.

[11] Ibid., p. 7.

situations of problem solutions.[12]

In the West, technology is a part of the historicity of the world; but because it is compensation for the historicity of nature, it is compensation for the fallen state of nature and the deficient state of the human person and of nature that originated from the fall. It is, therefore, not surprising that the three essential hopes that the human race places in technology aim at the deficiencies that have come into nature through the fallen state of nature according to the religious interpretation: death, the shortage of resources, the shortage of living space and time, the deficiency that human existence is always linked to local places, and the shortage of effortlessness of communication in social relationships and of the communication and dissemination of knowledge.[13]

The Eastern religions, therefore, have not proved historically to be as open to the real technology of the economy and the social technology of the organization, because they do not recognize the historicity of human beings and nature following from the fall.[14] Their striving for realization of the common good and compensation for the shortages of human existence aim more at strategies of individual and intellectual technology, the spiritual technology of the renunciation of the self and of becoming self-less. Shivram S. Antarkar presents the striving for redemption of the Śramaṇa tradition of Buddhism and Jainism as striving for śrama (pronounced *shrama*) = self-effort, śama (pronounced *shama*) = self-control, and sama = equanimity.[15] Corresponding to the religious individualism and individual striving for redemption, there are individual spiritual techniques and strategies for overcoming the neediness of human life, which cause the real technology of the control of external nature to decrease in importance.

---

[12] Christoph Hubig, *Technik- und Wissenschaftsethik: ein Leitfaden*, 2nd. Ed. (Berlin: Springer, 1995), pp. 58ff. Cf. also Klaus Mainzer, *Computer – neue Flügel des Geistes?* (Berlin: de Gruyter, 1994).

[13] Annette Ohme-Reinicke speaks of "three great ideas of progress, which human beings have of technology and which lead to technology-euphoria: happiness through free movement, freedom through unrestricted communication, and the lengthening of life" ("Fortschritt als Provokation: Die Technik schiebt sich zwischen Mensch und Natur," *Neue Züricher Zeitung*, 24/25 March 2001, p. 55).

[14] T. R. Anantharaman points out the shortage of historical thought in Hinduism in his contribution to Volume 2, *The Origin and the Overcoming of Evil and Suffering in the World Religions*, of the series A Discourse of the World Religions (Dordrecht: Kluwer, 2001), pp. 100-12. Deepak Lal also emphasizes the significance of the doctrine of the fall and of original sin for furthering economic-technological progress and consequently the ascent of the West in Deepak Lal, *Unintended Consequences: The Impact of Factor Endowments, Culture, and Politics on Long-Run Economic Performance* (Cambridge, Mass: MIT Press, 1998), pp. 75-110 and 153-58.

[15] In this volume, pp. 101.

1.4. TECHNOLOGY AS THE EFFORT TO SAVE EFFORT: WESTERN AND EASTERN REAL AND INTELLECTUAL TECHNOLOGY

This comparison of Eastern and Western religions and civilizations says nothing about the religious and ethical level of the respective civilizations. It says for the time being only something about their technological and economic success. A civilization that places less emphasis on social and real technology than on the individual and intellectual technology of spirituality may stand higher religiously and spiritually. And a civilization of technology and of economic progress may be impoverished spiritually, precisely *because of* the alienation of its striving for salvation and the merely material realization of the common good.

As Ortega y Gasset has written, technology is "the effort to save effort." According to him, this effort leads to the creation of a "super-nature" or other nature, to a "reform of nature."[16] Technology, as a transformation of nature, in turn enables the historicity of nature to be recognized. The saving of effort through technology can bring it about that *all* effort is reduced, even intellectual and spiritual effort, and that the corresponding organs that are replaced and economized decline or atrophy – even that the organ to perceive the intellectual effort of someone who has not saved this effort declines and disappears.

The forms of the spirituality of the religions are frequently efforts to avoid a false effort. Spirituality is the effort to avoid a false effort of the loss of self in the external. It can be regarded as the effort to economize or completely to avoid an effort, and thus can often be more economical than the simple economy of the avoidance of efforts. Bernard Hodgson has pointed out that the economy of avoidance of needs in the face of scarce resources is more economical in many situations than the economic striving for the most economically possible fulfillment of these needs given scarce resources.[17]

If the desiring human subject and the world of objectivity characterized by scarcity oppose one another irreconcilably, so that the desires of the subject cannot be satisfied, then either the human desires or the relations of scarcity must be changed. The first strategy, the transformation of the material desires into spiritual goals that do not stand in conflict with those of other persons, is the specifically religious strategy of addressing the limitations of material existence. Forms and techniques of asceticism are components of all religions. Asceticism, as an individual technique of one's lifestyle, possesses a technical side, in addition to the spiritual side, just as the invention and realization of technological goals also frequently presupposes an ascetic lifestyle.[18] The effort to economize effort, which technology undertakes, is itself an effort.

Consequently, religion and technology exhibit more commonalities than

---

[16] J. Ortega y Gasset, *Meditación de la tecnica* (1933).

[17] Bernard Hodgson, *Economics as Moral Science* (Berlin: Springer, 2001).

[18] Sergey S. Horuzhy points this out in his contribution to this volume.

might at first appear. The religious lifestyle, with the objective of improving and rationalizing the individual life, and technological innovation, with the objective of making human life easier, are both reforms of nature, in one case, the reform of inner, human nature, and in the other case, the reform of external nature.[19]

In their awareness that the improvement of life and of the use of nature is possible only through reform and effort or by forms of asceticism, religion and technology resemble one another and differentiate themselves from magical-mythical thought. Ernst Cassirer and Arnold Gehlen have pointed out that technology could emerge only after moving beyond magical-mythical thought.[20] A commonality between high religion and technology also becomes visible here: Both arise only after the break with magical-mythological consciousness.

2. The Hopes of Technology to Transform Matter as the Transformation of Theological Hopes

2.1. TECHNOLOGY AND MAGIC

One can characterize magical-mythical thought by the hope to be able to influence the matter of the world directly by thought and without the aid of mechanics, chemism, or the genetics of biology, so that it produces what the person applying the magic desires. Alchemy, with its hope of producing a change of nature or matter by magic, is a basic model.

The concept of changing nature is a basic concept of both technology and religion. In general, however, religions reject the practice of magic. The interpretation of karma as transformation of the corporal nature of the human person in Hinduism and Buddhism and the interpretation of the Eucharist as transubstantiation and the bodily resurrection as transformation of matter in Christianity are not magical processes and are not under the control of humans by magic. The change of the karmic body and the karmic matter of the human person, which by his good or bad deeds lead either to a higher and better or a lower and worse state, cannot be caused by him by the practice of magic, but can only be brought

---

[19] Max Weber's thesis of the inner-worldly asceticism of the modern economy, technology, and economy as a transformation of monastic asceticism into the inner-worldly asceticism goes in this direction. Nevertheless, with him it remains unclear how the old monastic asceticism could have been the opposite of "inner-worldly," and thus "outer-worldly."

[20] Cf. E. Cassirer, "Form und Technik" (1930), in *Symbol, Technik, Sprache: Aufsätze aus den Jahren 1927-1933*, ed. E. W. Orth and J. N. Krois (Hamburg: Meiner, 1985), pp. 30-90, here p. 63; and A. Gehlen, *Die Seele im technischen Zeitalter* (Hamburg: Rowohlt, 1957), p. 15, and *Urmensch und Spätkultur*, 3rd Ed. (Bonn: Athenäum, 1975), Chaps. 43-45.

about by deeds, and thus through real effectiveness in the external world.[21]

The transformation of bread and wine in the Mass or worship service of the Catholic or Lutheran Church is, likewise, not caused by the magic of the priest or pastor, but instead, according to Christian faith, by God himself, who is seen as the only person with the magical ability to affect the matter directly by the spirit.

Transubstantiation as transformation of matter is a dream of technology. The transformation of matter should be performed controllably by technology. The development from the mechanical via the chemical to the genetic control of nature appears to lead technology ever closer to this goal. If genetic engineering makes if possible, by transformation of a gene, to compel an organism to produce a substance desired by the manipulator, insulin for instance, or something similar, for use in healing the complete organism, it would appear that one had come close to the magical and alchemical transformation of matter.[22] Nevertheless, in the natural sciences it is still the causal change of external actions and processes that produces the desired result, not a magical act of the spirit that directly influences the matter.

As the religions see it, the phenomenon of transformation remains a prerogative of God. In Christianity, not the human person, but God, is the Lord of the transformation of the bread into resurrected body; in Hinduism it is the law of karma that brings about the materialization of the human person in the karmic body of the reincarnation and that is not at the technological disposal of the human person. The human person is not the free manipulator of karma.

Serious technology recognizes the limits and the methodology of its ability to transform matter and nature. It is, however, not to be overlooked that modern technology is co-determined in its goals by ideas of transformation that have theological origins and are meaningful only in their theological contexts. When the goals of technology turn into or are in danger of turning into the euphoria of technology, attributes always appear that are originally theological and originally restricted to God. This is the case when the goal of limitless communication of knowledge is confused with fantasies of omniscience, when the goal of over-

---

[21] On the transformation of karmic matter by actions in Indian thought, see the contribution of Shivram S. Antarkar to this volume.

[22] Ben Goertzel speaks of "magical new genetics" and expresses thereby his hope in the "magical effectiveness" of genetics – though completely without irony. His article is ambiguous: The latest genetic technology will compel the gene to action, "to its expression." But, on the other hand, "we do not know how we should interpret the code." The millions of molecules that join together under the influence of the genes should be decoded by the "artificial intelligence analysis of the genome data and by the automatic carrying out of biological experiments." On the other hand: "Gene therapy is a new approach to fighting against diseases that up to now has not been able to prove its practical use convincingly" ("Magische neue Genetik: Jetzt wächst zusammen, was zusammengehört: Die Computertechnologie bereitet den Weg zur Postgenombiologie," *Frankfurter Allgemeine Zeitung*, No. 145, 26 June 2001, p. 50).

coming space and time by limitless mobility is confused with hopes of omnipresence, and when the goal of the extension of life is confused with ideas of immortality.

2.2. IMMORTALITY THROUGH TECHNOLOGY

The theme of human immortality, to which a volume of its own of the series A Discourse of the World Religions, Volume 4, is dedicated, is a concern of both religion and technology. On the basis of their foresight of death, their "existence to the death," human beings are dominated by the problem of becoming immortal and the possibility of continuing to live after death, on one hand, or by the attainment of immortality through technology, on the other hand, as by hardly any other vital question.

The latest computer technology is obsessed with the idea of attaining human immortality by fusion with computers. All of my brain data would be saved on a chip and my body would be replaced by a computer, which would cost no more than $1,000 in about the year 2025.[23] I would store myself and gain immortality on a hard disk – and for less money than a Central European requires to live decently for a month. Bill Joy cites Danny Hillis: "I love my body no more and no less than anyone else; but if I can live to be two hundred years old with a body made of silicon, I'll accept it."[24]

One can ask here, on one hand, "Why be so modest?" Once we have created a hard disk as a body for ourselves, we can reproduce ourselves for all eternity with the suitable technology in ever newer computers. On the other hand, it must be objected that the continuity of the medium that consciousness uses for its maintenance, and thus the continuity of consciousness itself, is not guaranteed by this kind of technology. The moment of the nanosecond in which my self-consciousness changes from my body to the computer destroys the continuity of my self as a unity of mind and body. The tendency of technology to underestimate the human body, which has been mentioned above, is also apparent here.

2.3. EMBODIED INTELLIGENCE AS CRITIQUE OF THE SPIRITUALISTIC TENDENCIES OF ARTIFICIAL INTELLIGENCE RESEARCH

Technological utopias speak of the reconstruction of the human person and of the replacement of our bodily organs by machines that will ensure us of immor-

---

[23] Bill Joy, "Warum die Zukunft uns nicht braucht: Die mächtigsten Technologien des 21. Jahrhunderts – Robotik, Gentechnik und Nanotechnologie – machen den Menschen zur gefährdeten Art," *Frankfurter Allgemeine Zeitung*, 6 June 2000, pp. 49-50, here p. 50.

[24] Joy, p. 49.

tality, because they will be independent of the age of the body.[25] Such a utopia is possible only if one completely removes thought, intelligence, and consciousness from the body and imagines the consciousness, as in Cartesianism, to be a bodiless unity.[26] Precisely this removability of the mind from the nature of the body is disputed, however, among advanced advocates of technology. In their dissent from the "technological idealism" of those who are euphoric about artificial intelligence, they move in the vicinity of the religions' conviction of the unity of mind and body.

Computer scientist and artificial intelligence researcher Rolf Pfeifer considers the idea that intelligence is only a characteristic of calculating machines and brains to be mistaken: Intelligence is not identical with the brain, but is instead a characteristic of the whole organism.[27] The American artificial intelligence and robotics researcher Rodney A. Brooks points out that intelligence must be connected to the external world. The body, however, is the mediation between the intelligence and consciousness of the human person and the external world and, therefore, is not only "external" to consciousness. Intelligence requires the body in order to interact with the world. Brooks speaks of "embodied intelligence."[28]

The idea of attaining human immortality by the increasing substitution of organs by machines finds its limits at the identity of mental and bodily experience in the hylomorphic human person. A human being that consists only of mechanical organs or whose experience is only saved on a hard disk is not only bodily, but also mentally no longer identical to the original individual. Human beings of the future will wish to remain "Predominantly-Original-Substratum-Persons"[29] – and they must, because otherwise they will no longer be identical with themselves.

Another problem concerns the economic and ecological side of the immor-

---

[25] Cf. Villö Huszai, "Der Kampf um die Vorherrschaft der Intelligenzen: Die technische und literarische Phantasie vom Maschinenmenschen," *Neue Züricher Zeitung*, 24/25 March 2001, p. 57; and Ray Kurzweil, *The Age of Spiritual Machines: How we will live, work and think in the new age of intelligent machines* (London: Orion Business, 1999).

[26] Cf. for instance Ray Kurzweil, "Die Maschinen werden uns davon überzeugen können, daß sie Menschen sind: Nur weil Europa die technologische Revolution verschläft, muß nicht die ganze Welt vor sich hin träumen," *Frankfurter Allgemeine Zeitung*, 5 July 2000, p. 51: "We are gaining the power over life and death.... Someone who buys a new computer today does not dispose of the old data, but instead transfers it. Thus, software with its data has a life expectancy that does not depend upon the hardware. Our understanding of life and death may not permit the data of the human mind, which, in addition to the genetic inheritance, also contains our memory, our abilities, our personalities, to die with the hardware. Therefore, we will have to separate software and hardware. That does not mean that the life of our data would last from now on eternally. They live as long as they are of significance to someone.

[27] Cited by Annette Ohme-Reinicke, "Fortschritt als Provokation."

[28] Cf. Rodney A. Brooks, "Das Fleisch und die Maschine: Wie die neuen Technologien den Menschen verändern werden," *Frankfurter Allgemeine Zeitung*, 4 September 2000, p. 49; and Rodney A. Brooks, *Embodied Intelligence* (Cambridge, Mass.: MIT Press, forthcoming).

[29] Cf. Villö Huszai, "Der Kampf um die Vorherrschaft der Intelligenzen."

tality project, the project of "immortality by machines." Jaron Lanier remarks that almost-immortality will be possible only for the ultra-rich, because the mechanical substitution of organs will be extremely expensive and there will not be enough available space on the earth, if human beings become almost immortal *and* continue to reproduce. The high price of immortality leads him to ask: "In fifty years, will one consider the ultra-rich and everyone else to belong to the same species?" And he continues: "One day the richest among us will become almost immortal, which means they will be virtual gods in comparison to the rest of humanity."[30]

3. Total Control of Evolution by Science and Technology?

The technological possibilities open to human beings have always raised for the religious world-interpretation the question of the relationship between the normativeness of the created order, as understood in the concept of creation, and the liberty of human persons in their technological co-creation. Are we free to use technology, not only to continue, but also to surpass creation?

3.1. THE PROBLEM OF RELEASING SELF-REPLICATING STRUCTURES

The new biological and information technologies pose this question with renewed intensity, because, on one hand, they enormously increase human power over living things and over the mind and, on the other hand, they release or threaten to release self-replicating technologies that can become independent and reproduce themselves independently of the will of their creators. Intervention in the process of replication, however, is always more serious than the manipulation of existing entities, because it influences new realities and future replications, by which the good or the bad can reproduce and propagate itself.

Even more serious is the production of something completely new, which has no example in nature and can control and manipulate its own replication. A computer virus that can replicate itself in the "host computer" in order to paralyze many other computers, as the "love bug" attempted to do throughout the world in the spring of 2000, is much more dangerous than a simple virus that paralyzes only one computer.

Finally, computer programs that can reprogram themselves at higher levels independently of human supervision are even more dangerous. Technologically

---

[30] Jaron Lanier, "Aus den Ruinen unserer Zeit wächst ein zweiter Kapitalismus: Bill Joy fürchtet sich vor dummen Computern, ich fürchte mich vor dummer Software – die neuen Technologien werden eine frühindustrielle Klassengesellschaft erzeugen," *Frankfurter Allgemeine Zeitung*, 12 July 2000, p. 51.

self-reproducing and spreading techno-beings[31] could replicate themselves at such a speed and to such an extent that they could drive the human species out of the limited common biotope of the earth. Mechanical beings would become the rulers of nature and human beings, the former rulers, would become an extinct species. Technology would become, via such intermediate beings between humans and robots, a direct partner of biological evolution.

3.2. EVOLUTIONARY DISPLACEMENT OF HUMANS BY MACHINES?

The theme of the EXPO 2000, "Humankind, Nature, Technology," identifies evolution's partners, as the secular world view and evolutionism see them: nature, humans, and technology. "In the game of life and evolution there are three players at the table: human beings, nature, and machines," George Dyson writes.[32] The world view of the religions recognizes in addition to the triad of humankind, nature, and technology, the quaternity of God, humankind, nature, and technology." In the interpretation of the religions, not three, but, if one wishes, four players sit at the table, and the religions do not interpret these players as gamblers or as selection enemies that supplant one another, but as participants and cooperative partners. Dyson continues in his book *Darwin among the Machines*: "I am firmly on the side of nature. But nature, I suspect, is on the side of the machines."[33]

One could interpret the proposition that nature is on the side of the machines to mean that in the secular world view nature is an opportunist that always devotes itself to the stronger party. It will take the side of the strongest, the machines. For just as human beings as creatures have taken over the rule of God as the creator in the process of scientific-technological progress, the machines, the creatures of human beings, will take control from us, the creators of the machines, and instead of us become the ruling "people." To be sure, there is the opposing view that the work can never take over the role of its author and depose him: "We must not be afraid of machines, for we, the human machines, will always be a step ahead of them, the mechanical machines. We will not download ourselves, but will instead turn into machines."[34] Brooks points out correctly the prerogative and the superiority of the author to be ahead of the

---

[31] George B. Dyson, *Darwin Among the Machines: The Evolution of Global Intelligence*, (Harmondsworth: Penguin, 1999), p. 32, points out the difference between replication in terms of information technology and the replication of organisms: With the replication of information, information and metabolism are no longer a unity in an organism, but are instead independent of one another, while in organisms replication and metabolism are inseparably connected. If the organism dies, so does the information within it.

[32] Ibid., p. ix.

[33] Ibid. It is, however, unclear whether Dyson is not in fact on the side of the machines when he writes: "We are brothers and sisters of our machines" (p. x).

[34] R. A. Brooks, "Das Fleisch und die Maschine."

product. The author and the innovator is always a step ahead of his creature and imitator. This is also the basis for the hope of the religions that the author of the universe will always be a step ahead of his creatures and products.

Evolutionism in turn must fear that in the game and the struggle for survival, nature will be on the side of the machines, if they prove to be fitter and more capable of adaptation than humans. Nature will then no longer need humans; evolution will surpass us to the level of anthropoids and supercomputer beings.

The fact that evolution can go beyond humans also makes it difficult for evolutionism simply to demand that humans must only take evolution in the hand and may no longer leave it to chance.[35] This demand would be understandable, if one could be sure that human beings know better than evolution. However, if this is not certain – and it is not – the danger exists that evolution, with or without the intervention of humans in it, will go beyond us. If evolution, however, will go beyond humans, why should we still take part in our own deposition? Would it not be better for humans to leave their own deposition to chance than to contribute to it? It appears that the debate about central planning or evolutionary development, which characterized the opposition between central-planning economists and evolutionary market process theorists, is repeated in the relationship to nature.

The world religions also assume that nature is *not only* on the side of human beings. It is, instead, at the same time their opponent. The religions assume that nature, which was originally a friend of humanity, has, as a consequence of a fall or of evil, turned against us and now also behaves toward us with hostility. The world religions assume, however, that God is on the side of humanity and that with God's help human persons will also withstand an alliance of nature and machines. They also assume that nature needs human persons in order to complete itself, and that we must help it to achieve this completion, so that we can arrive at a state of eternal peace between humanity and nature.

3.3. SELF-ATTRIBUTION OF DIVINE QUALITIES THROUGH HYPER-TECHNOLOGY

It must not be overlooked that in the debate about the future of humanity, nature, and technology, the current state of information technology, the supercom-

---

[35] Cf. Georg H. Fey and Carl Friedrich Gethmann, "Wir dürfen unsere Evolution nicht dem Zufall überlassen: Der Mensch hat die Pflicht, sein genetisches Schicksal mit zu gestalten": *Frankfurter Allgemeine Zeitung*, 30 January 2001, p. 49. If one reads Fey and Gethmann's article more closely, it is not all of evolution that they wish to control, but particular, thoroughly well-defined evolutionary processes. They claim "that humans not only may co-form evolutionary processes in the direction of the improvement of their living conditions, but also should do so." It is difficult to see who would disagree! This demand has little to do with the demand for total control of evolution that no longer leaves anything in it to chance.

puter, nanotechnology, and the Internet, but also biotechnology,[36] increasingly claim attributes that one must call "theological." If, for instance, computer scientists such as Ray Kurzweil assume that nanotechnology, in association with genetic technology, will heal all diseases, that computers will make personal immortality possible, and that, with the supercomputers of the future, knowledge, events, and data will no longer be forgotten, it can be seen that religious promises are being repeated in the form of prophecies of technological progress.

If one adds that the perfect Internet amounts to overcoming space and time completely and produces the unity of center and periphery, in which the periphery immediately possesses all knowledge that is available to the center, divine attributes once again become visible. God is omniscient. He is not limited by space and time. He is the unity of periphery and center. God's omniscience, his omnipresence, and sempiternity are, however, inseparable from his omnibenevolence or perfect moral goodness, a quality which, unfortunately, we cannot ascribe to the Internet. How we should think about the theological attributes of the networks of knowledge that are created and maintained by human beings is a technological, ethical, and theological problem.[37]

3.4. THE EMPHASIS ON THE INNER LIMITS OF TECHNOLOGY AND OF THE CONTROL OF NATURE IN THE RELIGIONS

Religions can propose models of the normativeness of nature, both external nature and human nature. If they are honest with themselves, however, they recognize that they necessarily can propose the limits of technology only with a certain indefiniteness. The limits of technology can be determined only with a

---

[36] Cf. James D. Watson, "The Ethik des Genoms: Warum wir Gott nicht mehr die Zukunft des Menschen überlassen dürfen," *Frankfurter Allgemeine Zeitung*, 26 September 2000, p. 55. Even Hubert Markl, who might otherwise agree with Watson to a great extent, speaks of "biotheological exaggerations" in the claims of genetic research to have decoded the genome like a book ("Von Caesar lernen heißt forschen lernen: Die Menschenwürde gebietet, dem Rubikon ständig ein neues Bett zu bahnen: Der Flut der Erkenntnis können vatikanische Machansprüche keinen Einhalt gebieten," *Frankfurter Allgemeine Zeitung*, 25 June 2001, p. 52). It is noteworthy that both Watson and Markl argue in these two articles for the right to kill embryos, as if this right represented the core of research freedom. Cf. also Frank Schirrmacher's criticism of this article and of Markl's thesis that human dignity is culturally attributable and, therefore, divisible ("Bürger Markl: Der Präsident der Max-Planck-Gesellschaft treibt Kultur," *Frankfurter Allgemeine Zeitung*, 26 June 2001, p. 47).

[37] The Internet and the media represent not primarily the ubiquity of knowledge, but an extension of sense and perception. Marshall McLuhan has interpreted the media as expansion of human sense and perception and therefore as the basis of the possibility of a global community of sense and perception (*Understanding Media: The Extensions of Man* [New York: McGraw-Hill, 1964; 8th Ed., Cambridge, Mass.: MIT Press, 1999]). This more modest interpretation of information technology as the global expansion of perception agrees more with the phenomenon of globalization than does the interpretation of the Internet and the information community as the global expansion of actual knowledge.

certain carefulness and openness, because the religions themselves determine the human person as an open creation, as a bridge to the divine, whose limits, therefore, are themselves open, not fixed. Since, according to the world religions, human persons are open to transcendence, they transcend themselves infinitely. The determination of the limits of human self-transcendence by technology is, therefore, not a simple determination by external limits, but a determination by the internal limits that leave open the potential of the human person for self-transcendence and the potential of nature for its completion and peace with humanity.

The boundaries between a technological reform of nature and the magical omnipotence dreams of technology are set by the respect for the boundaries of the transformations of nature by technology. A technology that regards nature only as the matrix of its total transformation, which from its substratum sets no limits for the human person in advance, will not lead to an improvement of the creation. Since they regard the origin of nature as divine and as standing above the human person, the religions demand that nature remains "Predominantly-Original-Substratum-Nature," and they emphasize the karma-nature of human action in its effects on external, material nature. Bad actions worsen not only the moral nature of the human person, but also the natural nature of nature. Modern technology is not interested in understanding such a karma-effect of technology on nature. It is in danger of regarding nature as in fact the infinitely available matrix of human action. It could be, however, that religions, with their knowledge of the effect of the spirit and of human action on nature, which has been tested through the ages, are wiser than technologies.

Translated from the German by David W. Lutz

HUMANKIND'S RELATIONSHIP WITH NATURE AND PARTICIPATION IN THE PROCESS OF CREATION THROUGH TECHNOLOGY IN THE VIEW OF JUDAISM

Micha Brumlik

1. Western Critique of Judaism

The Church Father Tertullian (160-225), like many others who wished to strengthen the orthodox faith of the Church, was concerned with currents in the emerging Church considered to be heretical, including the doctrine (effective at the time of Hadrian) of Marcion, who made a distinction between the Christ of the Gospels and "the one whom the Creator God destined for transferring Judaism into its last state and who will someday return." The Gnostic critique of the Creator God of the Hebrew Bible has a history of nearly two thousand years and lives on a Platonic motif, which in this tradition was read contrary to its original sense. In the *Timaeus*, in the speech of the dialogue participant with the same name, Plato develops an extensive cosmic speculation, in which a creator with the name of "demiurge" creates the cosmos in accordance with present examples or models, according to the discipline of a craftsman. Finding this originator and father of the universe would be just as difficult as making him known. Gnostic speculation later identified this demiurge with the Creator God of the Hebrew Bible, but also concluded from the experience of evil in the world that its creator must have been malicious. This idea-figure shaped all of Western history up to Martin Heidegger, who postulated a God who should liberate existing entities from the abuse of the machinations. Possibly, the identification of the Creator God and the merely technically-effective demiurge led to an anti-Judaic idea-figure in such a way that the God of the Hebrew Bible and those who professed him, the Jews, became the initiators of a process of domination, according to which human beings are the enemies of nature.

The young Hegel's critique of Judaism is along these lines. The positivity of (Jewish) religion, which Hegel, with thoroughly historical concepts, again and again calls "condition" (*Zustand*), assumes the characteristic of a super-historical, persisting condition in his analysis. The character of Judaism reveals itself from the beginning of its history, which Hegel, like the Jewish tradition itself, begins with Abraham. Abraham's struggles, defeats, and triumphs bear

P. Koslowski (eds), Nature and Technology in the World Religions, 18–28.

witness to the history of an independence without love, of the will to an independence that seeks a new home, completely without resentment, without being
insulted and expelled. Hegel attempts to find evidence in Abraham's life of a
fundamental rejection of nature – in the details of his nomadic existence, in his
alleged inability to cultivate and improve the appearance of the land on which
he grazed, in his digging of wells and quarrels over pastures, in his unwilling-
ness to bless the places where God appeared to him – an attitude for which Hegel also reproached historical Christianity, with its eradication of Germanic religion.[1] Abraham was "a stranger upon the earth,"[2] and if his character shaped the
character of his nation, it is also true of the Jewish nation that its attitude toward
the world is fundamentally one of alienation. Since Hegel, in selective reading
of the Old Testament, lets the creation story begin only with the Flood, the
world and nature become simply an opposing principle for Abraham, something
"carried by a foreign God,"[3] Abraham's will to independence and freedom, tied
to an indifference towards nature as his place of origin and home, which results
from the renunciation of love, leads to his subjugation of it, and leaves him with
nothing more from this world than the means of subsistence, in order to let
everything else become unimportant, and to place him in security with respect
to it.[4] Therefore, according to Hegel, nature becomes the infinite object and the
relationship to it necessarily becomes one of "domination" (*Beherrschung*).
Thus the young Hegel already conceived a "dialectic of enlightenment" as the
domination of nature, and explained it in terms of the Jewish relationship to
God.[5] Hegel paid tribute here to a Romantic Zeitgeist. The rediscovery of nature
as a moral principle, the growing critique of Kant's moralism, and the rejection
of Jacobinism and its terrorist crowds let Hegel construe the biblical Abraham
as a precursor of the "absolute freedom" that was criticized later in phenomenology. Abraham – that is the epitome of the renunciation of love! The discussion of the sacrifice of Isaac, which began with Kant and was repeated again
and again from Kierkegaard to Derrida,[6] finds a first high point with Hegel:

> He could love nothing, even the only love that he had, for his son and his hope of
> posterity, the only way to extend his existence, the only kind of immortality that

---

[1] G. W. F. Hegel, "Frühe Schriften," in Hegel, *Werke*, ed. Eva Moldenhauer (Frankfurt: Suhrkamp), Vol. I, p. 197.

[2] *Ibid.*, p. 278.

[3] *Ibid.*, p. 279.

[4] *Ibid.*, p. 279.

[5] C. Jamme, "Jedes Lieblose ist Gewalt: Der junge Hegel, Hölderlin und die Dialektik der Aufklärung," in C. Jamme and H. Schneider, eds., *Der Weg zum System: Materialien zum jungen Hegel* (Frankfurt: Suhrkamp, 1990), pp. 130-71.

[6] S. Kierkegaard, *Fear and Trembling*, trans. H. V. Hong and E. H. Hong (Princeton: Princeton University Press, 1983); J. Derrida, *The Gift of Death*, trans. D. Willis (Chicago: University of Chicago Press, 1995).

he knew and hoped for, could force him, disturb his disposition of self-isolation from everything, and set it in unrest. This went so far one time that he also wanted to destroy this love and was reassured only through the awareness of the feeling that this love was only strong enough to allow him the ability to slaughter the beloved son with his own hand.[7]

Abraham's love, which the young Hegel understood to be the typical Jewish kind of love, is self-seeking, related only to the extension or preservation of one's own person. This selfishness terminates in contempt of the world and nature, in – one could say – a universalism of negation, which necessarily led to the conviction that one's own God was not only the nearest and favored God, but also the only God, and consequently that the Jews were the only people who had a God at all.

The autonomy based on self-seeking independence, with the renunciation of love, worked itself out further for Hegel in the liberation experience that should be characterized not only for the Western religions, but also for the freedom semantics of modernity, the Exodus story. Consistently with his presuppositions, however, Hegel can tell this story as nothing other than a failure. It will be obvious to anyone with a sense of history, however, that the fallacious interpretation of the Exodus as an unsuccessful emancipation story does justice neither to the biblical liberation experience nor to modern emancipation thinking. To be sure, if it is permissible to read the "Exodus" positively as a great story of modern liberation,[8] it is also fundamentally legitimate to depict it as a story of unsuccessful emancipation. Accordingly, the legislation imposed by Moses on the Israelites was supported by a principle that permitted only a servile consciousness of reward and punishment to be taught.

The varying – sometimes criticizing, sometimes praising – assessment of this idea of God does not permit the problematic nature of its basic structure to be forgotten:

> The infinite object, the epitome of all truth and all relationships, thus actually the only infinite subject, since it can be called an object insofar as the human person with his given life is presupposed and is called the living, the absolute subject – the only synthesis and the antitheses, so to speak, are the Jewish people, on one hand, and the entire remainder of the human race and the world, on the other hand.[9]

Since Hegel took biblical creation theology seriously, the God worshiped as infinite becomes the infinite, living – and in addition the only – subject, in contrast to everything finite, and becomes at the same time void, something that is

---

[7] Hegel, p. 279.
[8] M. Walzer, *Exodus and Revolution* (New York: Basic Books, 1985).
[9] Hegel, p. 283.

"without content and empty, without life, not even dead."[10] Hegel, therefore, attempts nothing less than a speculative derivation of the "soul of the Jewish nationality, of the *odium generis humani*."[11] The identification of the Jews with the infinite, living God devalues the world and the human persons living in it and leaves them with no relationship to this environment other than that of physical dependence, which weakens its own life to the level of bestial existence. God's guarantee of a secure life in the promised land does not go beyond it. The "eternal" values of honor, freedom, and beauty had to remain foreign to the Jews, because of their banishment by the infinite. Moses impressed his seal on this God relationship: "He brought the idea of himself before the servile spirit, the fear of physical power."[12] Hegel does not grow weary of describing dependency and servitude as basic features of the Jewish relationship to God, the world, and human persons.

2. Judaism and Creation

It actually belongs to the liturgical obligations of devout Jews on Friday evenings to commemorate the creation of the world and the liberation from Egypt at the same time in blessings:

> Blessed art thou, the Eternal, our God, King of the Universe, who hath sanctified us with his commandments, and found pleasure in us, and caused us to inherit his holy Sabbath in love and favor, as a memorial of the work of creation; for that day ranks first amongst the holy convocations in remembrance of the departure from Egypt....

The two events, creation and liberation, are related to one another and can be neither conceived nor understood apart from one another. Therefore, any perspective that would oppose the creation of the world and redemption or grace to one another is ruled out from the start. On the contrary, the liberation story sheds light on the creation, while the good of the creation willed by God attests the possibility of liberation.

Although thus – indisputably – God's action in the Book of Genesis is portrayed according to the model of the productive craftsman, or even of the ruler enjoining through his commanding word, it can be seen that the relationship to the world and to nature developed there is not one of instrumental rationality. Appropriate critique has oriented itself above all to the command of God in Genesis 1,28 of a fruitful human race according to his will, translated by Luther

---

[10] *Ibid.*, p. 283.
[11] *Ibid.*, p. 293.
[12] *Ibid.*, p. 288.

thus: "And God blessed them and said to them: Be fruitful and multiply and fill the earth and subjugate it." (*"Und Gott segnete sie und sprach zu ihnen: Seid fruchtbar und mehrt euch und füllt die Erde und macht sie euch untertan."*) In the German translation by Martin Buber and Franz Rosenzweig, which is more faithful to the spirit of the Hebrew language, the same verse reads: "God blessed them, God said to them: Be fruitful and multiply and fill this earth and make it yours." (*"Gott segnete sie, Gott sprach zu ihnen: Fruchtet und mehr euch und füllt diese Erde und bemächtigt Euch ihrer."*) The Hebrew word for "subjugate" (German, *untertan machen*) is *kibschu*, which literally means "conquer." The "earth" spoken of here is characterized in the Hebrew as *haaretz*, which means "land" in contrast to "sky" and "ocean." Thus, translated literally, the humans are told to conquer the land and then, in the continuation of the verse, to expel fish and birds. Buber and Rosenzweig translate this as "Rule over the fish of the sea" (*"Schaltet über das Fischvolk des Meeres"*). The Greek-language Septuagint – originating in Alexandria in the second century B.C. – translates the Hebrew *kibschu* with *katakyrieusate*, which means "subdue" (German, *unterwerfen*).

Thus it can be determined as a first result that the accusation of a technological seizure of the earth by the commission of the Creator God, recited from Luther until the civilization critique of the 1920s and 1930s, even widely until the end of the twentieth century, is to be attributed either to malicious misunderstanding or to mistranslation. The experiences of hydraulic, water-building societies of the Middle East in the first half of the first millennium B.C., particularly in Babylon, in which the Book of Genesis probably originated in the sixth century B.C., are fundamentally different from those of a Hellenistic – Egyptian large city, such as Alexandria in the second century. While *kibschu* names an extremely concrete process of settlement – for instance, taking land and building dikes along the North Sea – the Greek *katakyrieusate* actually identifies a social relationship: after all, *kyrios* was the monarchical epithet not only of Zeus as king of a hierarchy of gods, but also as the lord of marriage, as well as the kingly sovereign over a territory. It must be admitted, of course, that the medieval Jewish exegesis, fed by Talmudic traditions, still followed the sovereignty model. Thus the commentator Raschi (1040-1105) of Worms, in relation to the Talmudic and midraschic sources, interpreted *kibschu*: "to teach you that the man rules over the wife, that she not always leaves the house; and furthermore to teach you that the man, whose role is to rule, not the wife, is obligated to reproduction."[13]

Terms of technological-poietic acts in the narrower sense are found in the Book of Genesis primarily in the story of the creation of the humans and the genealogical stories of Cain and his descendants.

---

[13] Raschi, *Kommentar zum Pentateuch*, (Basel: Goldschmidt, 1975), p. 5.

In the twenty-sixth verse of the first chapter, God invites himself to create (*naasseh*) a man "according to our image and created them in his image" – possibly a fundamental "technological" progress is described here. In the second creation account (Gen. 2,7), "God created (*wajizer*) the man out of dust," while he later used the rib taken from the man to make (*wajiwen*) a woman (Gen. 2,22). The literal translation of *jizer* is "to produce," while *jiwen* means "to build." In the Septuagint, God invites himself in Genesis 1,26 to a *poiesomen*, while in 2,7 it reads *eplasen* (to form) and in 2,22 *oikodomesen* (to build). With Adam's sons and their quarrel, the murder of the herdsman Abel by the farmer Cain permits the Genesis story to begin the dialectic of human history.

Cain was a crop farmer, an *owed adama*, where *awodah* always means "service," even worship (of God) service, and *adama* does not mean here land in general, but mother earth. Jabal, a descendent of Cain and son of Lamech and Adah, was the father of all who dwell in tents and own livestock. Jubal, likewise son of Lamech and Adah, was the father of all who play the flute and zither. Tubal-cain, son of Lamech and Zillah, was a blacksmith and made all kinds of bronze and iron tools (Gen. 4,20-22). Finally, Noah, who was commanded by God to "make" (*laassoth*) an ark, as well as the inhabitants of Babel, who prepared to burn bricks in order to build the tower, are likewise engaged in productive acts.

The commentator Raschi imparts to Jabal, Jubal, and Tubal-cain that the building of the tents and the musical instruments served the worship of idols and that Tubal-cain (whose name is etymologically related to the term "seasoning") seasoned Cain's murderous act by the production of weapons. The sharpening of copper and iron, however, is associated with sharpening the view toward God. With the building of the Tower of Babel, the medieval expositor says that especially the calling clause *hawu* always has the meaning "that one prepares and unites oneself to a work or a plan or to carrying o a load."[14]

A first glance at technological-poietic concepts, as they are contained in the central Jewish revelation text, the Torah, thus produces a historical context that is shaped by a life-world that has indeed already experienced the centralization of advanced civilization, but is nevertheless still so far bound up with direct interaction with nature, a farming and nomadic way of life, that the relationship with the world practiced there does not aim directly at subjugation, but at taking possession and, furthermore – as Walter Benjamin pointed out much later in his interpretation of the creation story – is from the beginning linguistically transmitted and indeed not only in the form of imperatives, but also and particularly in the form of vocatives; God indeed names the light "becoming" in the first creation account, but later calls it "day." "All of nature," according to Benjamin:

---

[14] *Ibid.*, p. 14.

insofar as it transmits itself, communicates itself in language, and thus in the end in human persons. Therefore, he is the Lord of nature and can name all things. Only through the linguistic character of things does he arrive from himself to their knowledge – in naming. God's creation completes itself as things receive their names from men, from whom language speaks only in names.[15]

Insofar as, in relation to the Gnostic critique of the Creator God, technologically mediated world relationships are actually to be assumed, they nevertheless appear in a surprisingly varied and differentiated form. *Laassot – poeiein* – "to do," *lejazer – plattein* – "to form," and *lejawen – oikodomein* – "to build." While the Septuagint still reconstructed these differences accurately, Luther, as a man of modernity and, therefore, of a now truly technological relationship with nature, speaks in Genesis 1,26 and 2,7 of "making" (*machen*) and in 2,22 of "building" (*baute*). It was Hannah Arendt, who, with reference to Aristotle, pointed out the distinctions between *poiesis* (to work), *praxis* (to act), and *techne* (to produce). Accordingly, *poiesis* can actually be understood as "to act, to work," in the most general sense, while *techne* means (craftwork) production. With the question of the relationship of nature and technology in Judaism, it should be noted, nevertheless, that at least Greek-speaking Judaism did not know this term, when it concerns the relationship of God and nature. Equally, however, it was not in a position to name the special meaning of *bara*, "to create," in the first verse of Genesis with a term of its own, but likewise translated it as *epoiesen*.

3. The Sabbath as Relationship with the World

The typology and specificity of the Jewish relationship to nature can be developed, accordingly, only out of the interpretation of the creation intended in the Book of Genesis, from which, as a first result, it is the case that is was performed by a linguistic, interpretive act. In the act of creation, after looking at the creation, it is confirmed furthermore each time that it is good, and thus fundamentally affirmed in its existence. Nature, created by God, is thus not at all fallen or even sinful nature. At least as important as the linguistic *creatio ex nihilo*, the rhythmic classification performed according to days, and the fundamental affirmation, if not indeed more significant, is the end of the act of creation, as it is described in Genesis 2,1-3:

Thus heaven and the earth were completed, and all their multitude. And God completed the work that he had done on the seventh day, and rested on the sev-

---

[15] W. Benjamin, *Über Sprache überhaupt und über die Sprache des Menschen*, in Benjamin, *Gesammelte Schriften*, ed. R. Tiedemann, Vol. II, 1 (Frankfurt: Suhrkamp, 1980), p. 144.

enth day from all of the work that he had done. And God blessed the seventh day and hallowed it, for God rested on the seventh day from all of the work that he had done to finish the creation.

The idea of the Sabbath has been emphasized with justification again and again, and especially today, as an essential, social achievement – an achievement that was completely unknown in the entire ancient world, which to be sure knew many holidays. The rhythmic and continual return of a day of rest was already known in the eighth century in the Israeli and Jewish monarchies, though some Old Testament scholars also make a late dating here and trace back the establishment of the Sabbath to the experiences of exiled Jewish elites in the astronomically-trained Babylonian exile. It may be the case that the Babylonians understood a monthly new-moon day as a *sapattû* or an every seventh day, on which kingly actions were forbidden. An unambiguous genealogy of the *Schabbat* out of the combination of new-moon day and governmental-interval cannot, of course, be depicted historically.[16] Whatever its origin, however, the creation as a whole and the language in which it is expressed bows to none of the handwork-technical semantics related to the product of an artificial process, but is articulated in a completely different vocabulary. It is performed in a verb *bara*, which is used only for this event, and has an end, however, that ends not merely as a performance, but as a prosperous performance with an interruption, which places the Creator himself in the rhythm of his work. While labors simply end and Aristotelian *praxis* never creates and continues itself in its performance, while technological production is eventually concluded, the act of creation, which is a linguistic act, is concluded, completed, and ceremoniously interrupted. Interruption and completion join together in the biblical Shabbat and structure everyday life about the Sabbath commandment, as it is formulated in Exodus 23,12 and 34,21.

In the Sabbath commandment, as it is contained in the Book of Exodus, the interruption of work is subject to the clear establishment of social objectives: the Sabbath as the day on which one should celebrate, dedicated to the additional goal that all who perform the energy-draining activity of work can regenerate themselves. Exodus 34,12 prescribes even further that the weekly interruption breaks through the other rhythms of agricultural life still widespread at that time and is valid for the entire year. The rhythm of the vegetative farming life is replaced, consequently, by a social, nearly inclusive rhythm – the rhythm of human life and work replaces the rhythm of the annual seasons – it eventually can be seen that with the seven-day rhythm of the moon, the month, a celestial rhythm has replaced a terrestrial rhythm – admittedly: the social setting of goals is so obvious that the reference to celestial rhythms does not contribute much to an explanation. The concluding formulation of Deuteronomy 5,14-15 in the

---

[16] "Sabbath," *Encyclopedia Judaica*, Vol. 14 (Jerusalem: Keter), p. 562.

most recent part of the Torah contains the richest formulation of the Sabbath commandment:

> But the seventh day is the holiday of the Eternal One, your God; you shall per-
> form no work whatsoever then, you and your son, and your daughter, and your
> servant, and your maid, and your ox, and your ass, and all of your livestock, and
> the stranger within your gates, so that your servant and your maid may rest like
> you. And you shall remember that you were a servant in the land of Mizrajim,
> and the Eternal One, your God, delivered you from there with a strong hand and
> an outstretched arm; therefore, the Eternal One, your God, has commanded you
> to keep the Sabbath day.

On the basis of this commandment, a wealth of comprehensive legislation was enacted in ancient Israel, which included not only domestic, familial life, but the entire country. In Exodus 23,10-11 and Deuteronomy 15,1-11, it is pre- scribed that all debts are to forgiven every seventh year, that fields are to lie fallow, and that the harvest is to be used for feeding the poor. Seven Sabbath years, in turn, conclude in a year of Jubilee, during which the fields are given over in trusteeship to the priests and – to the extent that they were purchased from someone else – revert to the original owner. The complex legal conse- quences of these rules, which also have an effect on the possession of slaves, can be ignored here.[17]

In any case, it can be seen that in Jewish thought the relationship with nature is not built in accordance with the standards of the production of a workpiece, but – without working magically or anthropomorphically – in accordance with a complex social structure and a relationship of ruling, which is by no means characterized as a relationship of subjugation, but as a diverse, mutual relation- ship of obligation. This mutual relationship relates, however – especially con- cerning the question of the relationship to nature – to both living and non-living nature, and therefore to creation considered as a whole. It may be assumed to be well known that the ethics of ancient Israel, on the basis of the experience of bondage in Egypt, was inclusive and hence always also included the foreigners living in Israel, the *gerim*, as well as women and children. But, the fact that the Sabbath also holds true in the sense of an ethical obligation for livestock, for the ox and ass, even for the world of plants, reveals a world view that one could call "social cosmology." In contrast to mythical world views, those of a totemistic kind for instance, it is here not a matter of the cosmic equal rights of the worlds of gods, humans, animals, and plants, also not of a sacred taboo (as seems to me to be the case with the respect for cows in Indian religions), but of concretely formulated statutes. Contrary to the Gnostic critiques of a god who acts instru- mentally, who has subjugated the world and human beings to a unilateral utility-

---

[17] Cf. "Sabbatical Year and Jubilee!" *Encyclopedia Judaica*, Vol. 14, p. 574.

relationship, the nature relationship as it is developed in the Hebrew Bible proves to be ecological in the best sense. The creation, extending all the way to the earth, on which no permanent private property is ultimately permissible, belongs to God and is entrusted to human persons. His sovereignty works as a pledge of a just order, which opposes misuse and abuse and makes possible for human persons a use of the creation that enables their lives to be successful.

Contrary to the concept of isolated technological action, which is introduced here not only analytically, and the diverse concept of production of the Bible, which is always embedded in a social context, a fallacy, a misunderstanding, which is by no means fruitful, becomes distinct, the source of which is to be looked into conclusively. It has especially become clear, however, that the in fact neo-pagan (which does not have to be a insult) critique of monotheism as a nature-destroying idea is not only false, but nearly absurd. Evidence that polytheistic religions, merely because they worship divine, numinous powers in individual natural forces, would treat nature as a whole more carefully cannot be produced empirically, at least not with advanced cultures. And the extent to which one can attribute the technological subjugation of nature that characterizes modernity, disregarding specific circumstances, to the Judeo-Christian tradition is still to be determined. The results produced thus far do not substantiate it.

If, of course, it should be the case that the development of autonomous subjectivity per se, which can no longer be overcome by the forces of nature, is seen as the first step toward a relationship with nature pervaded by domination, as Horkheimer and Adorno did in their *Dialectic of Enlightenment*, the problem to be dealt with is not solved, but only postponed. That is to say, it was actually that autonomous subjectivity and that transcendent God, in the sense of a "dialectic of conservation", that made possible another relationship with nature, which was, at least in the biblical texts, if not directly poetic and romantic, nevertheless peaceful. It can be said *cum grano salis* that if the young Hegel had made an effort to read the Hebrew Bible in the original language, he could have spared himself the mental detours and revisions that eventually led him to his theory of the Jewish religion as a one of superiority.

4. Rabbinical Judaism

The Jewish religion is not identical to the religion of the Bible, but recognizes a second source of revelation, the Mischna, which according to tradition was likewise revealed as oral teaching at Sinai, was written down after the destruction of the temple, and finally was codified in the texts which we know as talmudic. They serve as the basis of the Judaism that has historically absorbed all other streams with the exception of Christianity: pharisaic-rabbinical Judaism. The ethics of pharisaic-rabbinical Judaism takes up what is said in the Book of Genesis about God's act of creation: that after the creation of the world he blessed his work. From this stimulus, rabbinical Judaism later abolished the separation of the profane and the sacred, which was until then common to all ancient religions, and thereby also placed everyday actions under the impulse of hallowing and blessing – just as God did at the end of the sixth day. With that, the modern assumption and praxis of an isolated instrumental act, which devoid of any sense aims only at the misuse of nature for arbitrary goals, is already contradicted to some extent. Whether the idea of a hollowing of action and conservation that is responsible to the creation can be reconstructed in the language of the profane, without relation to the transcendent God of the Bible who reveals himself, must remain open here. The Jewish philosopher Hans Jonas undertook this attempt in his *Principle of Responsibility* and experimented with the idea of demanding at least appealingly a rationally-based reverence for the miracle of nature. Most systems of ecological ethics, however, whether the have inherited religions of advanced civilizations or animistic religions, have broken down at this problem. If the bond between Creator and creation is cut and the Enlightenment has spread so far that faith in a Creator God no longer seems responsible, in which case it would be for the sake of a *sacrificium intellectus*, this reverence can now be established at best aesthetically, but that means: only aesthetically.

Translated from the German by David W. Lutz

THE WORLD AS CREATION AND CREATION AS A COSMOTHEANDRIC REALITY IN CHRISTIANITY

Francis X. D'Sa

1. Introduction

Every religious tradition is characterized by a specific understanding of the three realms: God, World, and Human. But not every tradition (for example, the religions of the Adivasis, Aboriginals of India) reflects thematically on them. Thus the Adivasi religions speak uninhibitedly of the World, Humans, and of the Highest Mystery. They see no problem in this, because they still live in a world of faith. The world of faith is so obvious and immediate to them that it is the perspective, though non-thematic, in which they experience, understand, and act. In such a case it is the world of faith that gives meaning; but as a matter of fact reflection does not belong to their horizon of meaning. The experience of faith is normative, on the one hand; but reflection on the world of faith is missing, on the other. The strength of such traditions is the immediacy of their faith-world. Their weakness, however, lies in the danger that they are not able to distinguish between faith and belief.

But the case is different with religious traditions where reflection plays an important role. A tradition of reflection testifies to the fact that the world of faith is no longer the centre of that tradition and that in some cases it is not always operative. In such cases reflection encounters the world of faith as a subject encounters its object. Reflection constitutes the centre, which poses questions and doubts, but the immediacy of the world of faith is conspicuous by its absence. Reflection demands that the world of faith give an account and a justification for its faith. Faith here is no longer taken for granted. The strength of such traditions lies in the fact that they discern before they believe. Their weakness lies in the fact that their reflection concerns beliefs, and so are not in contact with faith. The danger is that their exclusive concentration is on beliefs.

Besides that, there has to be a hermeneutic dimension in a mature tradition of reflection. Without a hermeneutic consciousness there is danger that religion gets caught up in the realm of reason. A hermeneutic accompaniment protects it from such a danger and sees to it that reflection constantly strives towards the wholeness of being-in-the-world. It does this by reminding us of the diverse presuppositions of being and thinking. The presuppositions of humans and their

P. Koslowski (eds), Nature and Technology in the World Religions, 29–46.
© 2001 *Kluwer Academic Publishers. Printed in the Netherlands.*

cultures are different; the same culture manifests in the course of its history different presuppositions. Because of this, the same thing is understood differently. This explains not only why there are different interpretations of the same religion, but also why it has to be so.

2. The Significance of the Belief in Creation

Most of the Christian traditions are reflection-traditions. To a great extent they are occupied with beliefs. They try to understand and explain everything, i.e. God, World, and Humans, from the viewpoint of their beliefs. Their beliefs are products of their Scripture and Tradition. The Christian tradition to which I belong has much to do with the Western tradition. In what follows, I wish to highlight the specificity of this tradition.

2.1. THE DISTINCTION BETWEEN CREATOR AND CREATION IS UNBRIDGEABLE

The Semitic traditions lay stress on the difference between Creator and created. The biblical tradition perceived itself as surrounded by divinizing personifications of natural forces and so distanced itself from any kind of divinization of nature. It did not tolerate any exception and regarded any failing in this respect as the greatest sin. When such failing did occur, the punishment was so severe that in the course of time the temptation became gradually weaker.[1] The first and greatest commandment of the biblical traditions highlights God's sovereignty unambiguously. The first commandment is the first, not because of the numerical order, but because it is the most important commandment. The chasm between God and creation was so exaggerated that it was in danger of separating God and creation. Major problems were connected with this. It is important to note that the difference between Creator and creation in the biblical traditions is unbridgeable.

This distinction was taken so seriously that it has gravely affected the Christian tradition. It appears that in the course of time it even affected the epistemological process. It is true that complex factors led to the separation of Creator and creation. However, the distinction between Creator and creation seems to have become the occasion for the separation of the knowing subject from the object that is to be known. The misunderstood distinction between Creator and creation appears to have been the prototype, as it were, for the distinction between Subject and Object. This in turn seems to have led to a metaphysics of Subject and Object. On such a metaphysics rests the whole realm of the

---

[1] Exodus 32.

sciences.

We know that history is not a linear, logical process. It has its own dynamic, which does not respect human intentions. Complex combinations of happenings, which no computer programme, however clever, could decipher, bring forth processes that determine the course of history. In such a history the environmental crisis is the world-expression of the separation of subject and object, where humans behave as subjects and treat the world as object. In spite of the appearance that the biblical tradition is responsible for this, it is important to look at the historical processes in order to find out what is to be done.

The subject-object perspective, which in itself is valid in a limited area, has come to determine today the whole realm of the epistemological process. What is reality, how do we reach reality, and which kind of knowledge is valid, are being determined by a scientific mentality that overlooks, neglects, or even denies the most important areas of be-ing.[2]

No one, whether scientist or a simple soul, can deny that our being-in-the-world is primarily an experience of our limitedness. Limitedness means that there are areas in life that we cannot manipulate at our pleasure. The Ultimate escapes us; we do not have the last word. The acknowledgement of the experience of limit is, ontologically speaking, nothing other than the acknowledgement of our total dependence. Total dependence may sound abstract; what is in effect experienced, however, is our limitedness on the ontological level and our vulnerability on the psychological level.

The acknowledgement of our limitedness, I submit, has to do with the first commandment. Not only our experience and our activity are limited; there is also something beyond our experience and activity, however we may name it, which we cannot control. The first commandment demands an acknowledgement of this realm, without which humans would have a fundamentally wrong self-understanding. Since any self-understanding has to do with meaning in life, the role of a right self-understanding cannot be underestimated. Hence one must not behave as if this were unimportant or irrelevant. True, religion and philosophy concentrate *ex professo* on this field. Still, it is fitting that humans concern themselves with and think about meaning in life. For it is a matter that has to do with the highest values and their role in life, where a one-sided scientific mentality cannot be of service.

---

[2] H.-G. Gadamer, *Wahrheit und Method: Grundzüge einer philosophischen Hermeneutik*, 4th Ed. (Tübingen: J.C.B. Mohr [P. Siebeck], 1974), p. xxvii: "Das Phänomen des Verstehens durchzieht nicht nur alle menschlichen Weltbezüge. Es hat auch innerhalb der Wissenschaft selbständige Geltung und widersetzt sich dem Versuch, sich in eine Methode der Wissenschaft umdeuten zu lassen. Die folgenden Untersuchungen knüpfen an diesen Widerstand an, der sich innerhalb der modernen Wissenschaft gegen den universalen Anspruch wissenschaftlicher Methode behauptet. Ihr Anliegen ist, Erfahrung von Wahrheit, die den Kontrollbereich wissenschaftlicher Methodik übersteigt, überall aufzusuchen, wo sie begegnet und auf die ihr eigene Legitimation zu befragen."

2.2. CREATION MEANS TOTAL DEPENDENCE ON THE GOD OF CREATION

Being created means being totally dependent upon God and God's Word and God's Presence. There is no area in which a creature would be self-dependent and independent of God. Creation means a complete, total in every respect dependence on the God of Creation. To believe in God means nothing else but to believe in the God of Creation. In the biblical tradition God is always the God of Creation. In other words, Creation means that God, no other divinity, is really the Life of all that is created. With Hans Kessler, we can formulate it thus: God is the one, without whom there is nothing.[3] This implies a very close relation between Creator and Creation. The existence of every single creature is a pure gift of the Creator. No creature can give itself existence, much less keep itself in existence. Creation in its very depths is dependent on the Creator.[4]

The other side of the belief in creation refers to the fact that all creatures are intimately connected with one another. Creation is a living unity in diversity. A human being, to say nothing of other creatures, can do nothing by him/herself. Not only breath, but every aspect of all life is the result of this belonging together. Appearances to the contrary, not even our breathing in and breathing out is a human achievement. We can breathe in and out, because it is made possible through mutual interdependence and belongingness.[5] Humans as trustees carry responsibility for the maintenance of this belongingness; they have to see to it that it is in no way destroyed.

Right up to our times, the biblical traditions have been blamed for the fact that humans have "subdued" the earth. For has not the Bible revealed the unambiguous command of God: "Subdue the earth, rule over the animals" (Gen 1, 26-28)?[6] A refutation of such views would be out of place in this paper; it would disrupt its whole scheme. It is enough to point out that serious studies

---

[3] H. Kessler, *Das Stöhnen der Natur: Plädoyer für eine Schöpfungsspiritualität und Schöpfungsethik* (Düsseldorf: Patmos, 1990), p. 52.

[4] Cf. J. Ratzinger, "Schöpfung," *Lexikon für Theologie und Kirche*, 2nd Ed., Vol. 9, 1967, p. 464: "Die Totalabhängigkeit, in der das geschaffene Sein, sofern es Sein hat, dem Schöpfer zugeordnet bleibt, wird von der traditionellen Theologie als 'Erhaltung' der Schöpfung bezeichnet, deren konkrete Bedeutung in der Lehre von der Mitwirkung Gottes näher durchreflektiert wird."

[5] H. Kessler, *Das Stöhnen der Natur*, p. 54 *emphasizes that the human person is created in solidarity with all beings.* He also cites the more recent literature, which has worked out the details of this aspect. The overemphasized anthropocentricity of the earlier Christian interpretations of creation makes room today for a solidarity of the human person with creation in its entirety. The anthropocentric tendency of Walter Kern is exemplary. See his "Zur theologischen Auslegung des Schöpfungsglaubens," in J. Feiner and M. Löhrer, eds., *Mysterium Salutis: Grundriss heilsgeschichtlicher Dogmatik*, Vol. II (Einsiedeln/Zürich/Köln: Benziger, 1967), pp. 529 ff.

[6] C. Amery, *Das Ende der Vorsehung: Die gnadenlosen Folgen des Christentums* (Reinbeck: Rowolt, 1972); E. Drewermann, *Der tödliche Fortschritt: Von der Zerstörung der Erde und des Menschen im Erbe des Christentums* (Regensburg: Pustet, 1983).

express a different conclusion. They show that such sweeping statements and suspicions are short-circuits that distort historical facts.[7]

2.3. CREATION IS AN ON-GOING HAPPENING

Creation is an on-going happening. It is not as if God first brings the universe into being and then the universe moves on its own; as if God had so created the world that it continues to work, as it were, on its own steam. Sometimes creation has been understood in this manner as a once and for all event. As a matter of fact, creation, which is the beginning of the history of salvation, leads to eschatology, which is its fulfilment. The continuously running history of salvation is a continuous creation.[8]

Clearly the biblical language of creation is a symbolic language, not an in-

---

[7] H. Kessler, *Das Stöhnen der Natur*, pp. 32-35. Kessler summarizes both the refutation of such opinions and the interpretation of the relevant biblical passages and the historical development as follows:

> Zunächst ist es historisch falsch, die Entwicklung von Naturwissenschaft, Technik und Naturobjektivierung im Abendland einfach auf die Voraussetzung des jüdisch-christlichen Schöpfungsglaubens (mit seiner Unterscheidung von Gott und Welt und seiner Entdivinisierung der Weltdinge zu Geschöpfen) zurückzuführen. Der jüdisch-christliche Schöpfungsglaube mußte überhaupt nicht zu solchen Entwicklungen führen, wie allein schon ein Blick auf das östliche oder das äthiopische Christentum erweist oder auch der Codex Justinians (529), der eine die Mitkreatur einbeziehende Humanität vertritt. Wie wir noch sehen werden, spielten ganz andere (geographische, kutlurelle usw.) Faktoren eine ausschlaggebende Rolle – neben der schon antiken Durchsetzung der anthropozentrisch-sophistischen statt der ionischen Natur philosophie... Sodann: Der biblische Schöpfungsauftrag wurde bis in die Neuzeit hinein in seinem ganzen Zusammenhang gelesen und so gerade nicht als Aufforderung zur selbst-herrlichen Instrumentalisierung und Ausbeutung der Natur verstanden. Ganz im Gegenteil. Von Beginn an spielte im Christentum zum Beispiel die Psalmenfrömmigkeit mit ihrem Lobpreis für alle Geschöpfe eine nicht zu unterschätzende Rolle – im Gottesdienst und im täglichen... Stundengebet: wer bei Tagesanbruch die "Laudes" anstimmte, konnte anschließend kaum die Natur – dazu noch im Gegensatz zur Auffassung der Zeit – als seelenlos empfinden. Allein schon von daher erstaunt es wenig, daß sich nicht nur im ostkirchlichen, sondern genauso im westkirchlichen Christentum eine reiche Fülle von Zeugnissen von Naturfrömmigkeit findet. Sie zeigen: hier wie dort hat man durchgängig in einer Schöpfer und ganze Schöpfung umfassenden Dreiecksbeziehung Gott-Mensch-Natur gedacht und diese nicht zu einer bloßen Beziehung Gott-Mensch bzw. gar Gott-Seele verengt; diese verhängnisvolle Verengung blieb wesentlich der westlichen Neuzeit vorbehalten. Historiker urteilen daher: "Wer nicht über die Gabe verfügt,,, 'Gras wachsen' zu hören, dürfte Mühe haben, vor der Neuzeit merkliche Unterschiede zwischen östlicher und westlicher Naturtheologie und Frömmigkeit wahrzunehmen.' Und auf die Art des erkenntnismäßigen Umgangs mit der Natur überhaupt bezogen: Es gibt in der Geschichte der Naturerkenntnis mit dem Eintritt des Christentums in die Mittelmeerwelt...keinen schroffen Bruch, sondern allenfalls Akzentverschiebungen.' Ganz entsprechend läßt sich eine durchgehende Kontinuität der abendländischen wissenschftlichen Tradition von der Zeit der Griechen bis zum 17. Jahrhundert" feststellen; erst dort ist ein tiefgehender Traditionsbruch zu erkennen."

[8] The natural scientist and theologian A. R. Peacocke expresses this as follows: "*Gott erschafft kontinuierlich; Gott ist semper creator. Gott ist der immanente Schöpfer, der in den Prozessen der natürlichen Ordnung und durch sie schöpferisch wirksam ist*" ("Natur und Gott: Für eine Theologie im Zeitalter der Wissenschaft," in *Gott, der Kosmos und die Freiheit: Biologie, Philosophie und Theologie im Gespräch*, ed. G. Fuchs and H. Kessler [Würzburg: Echter, 1996], p. 179).

formative language. Informative language is true when the information is correct. Such a language consists basically of concepts which have to be understood univocally, so that the various aspects can be verified (or falsified). In the case of symbolic language, this is not so; its truth is manifested in the transformation that it brings forth. Symbol language makes use of the symbols of an age in order to effect transformation. But it is easy to confuse one kind of language with the other. Symbol language has its own dynamics of communication. Hence, instead of interpreting symbol language literally, it is necessary to follow this dynamics.[9]

The creation narrative is not a report.[10] It is far from being a report about the beginning and the end of the history of salvation. In the Bible, the history of salvation is the background for all its narratives. Their theme is not the history of salvation; rather the history of salvation is the presupposition for all its narratives. What the narratives bring out is God's effective presence in history.[11] Because of this, the story of creation is the history of salvation. For we encounter God and salvation within, not outside, history. God's effective presence in history is a presence that keeps creation in being. Keeping creation in being means God continually brings creation into existence.

This has a number of consequences.

In the biblical tradition there is no such thing as the "world" in itself. What we have is a world that is continuously kept in being and pervaded by God's presence. Every creation and every happening *is*, because it finds itself in the Mystery of God. Outside of God there is nothing, there can be nothing. That means that the biblical belief in creation is a belief in the presence of God that works unceasingly in creation.

It should not be difficult to see what all this has to do with meaning in life. In the so-called good and bad times there is no reason for despair when belief in God's operative presence in the world is alive.[12] Nothing ever happens without

---

[9] See F. X. D'Sa, "Re-Searching the Divine: The World of Symbol and the Language of Metaphor," in J. Kozhamthadam, ed., *Interrelations and Interpretation: Philosophical Reflections on Science, Religion and Hermeneutics in Honour of Richard De Smet, S.J. and Jean de Marneffe, S.J.* (New Delhi: Intercultural Publications, 1997), pp. 141-73.

[10] See C. Westermann, *Creation* (London: SPCK, 1974), pp. 11 ff.

[11] Cf. for example D. Sperlings, "Israel's Religion in the Ancient Near East," in A. Green, ed., *Jewish Spirituality: From the Bible through the Middle Ages* (New York: Crossroad, 1987), p. 22: "The crucial difference between Israel and its neighbors was the emphasis of the Hebrews on the role of Yahweh as liberator, as redeemer from slavery, as donor of land and political sovereignty to a newly formed people. Because the exodus tradition was so pervasive in Israel, it made for a concentration on the role of Yahweh in history rather than in nature. Israel was not unique in crediting its God with historical concerns. But historical concerns had a far greater influence on the cult of Jahweh than on the cults of Israel's neighbors."

[12] See J. Ratzinger, "Schöpfung," in *Lexikon für Theologie und Kirche*, Vol. 9, p. 464: "Wenn Schöpfung allgemein die Logosbestimmtheit alles Wirklichen behauptet, so bedeutet die Aussage

God's will. Whatever happens is either directly willed or indirectly allowed by God. God makes use of everything for our salvation.[13]

This does not mean, however, that we remain passive and leave everything to God. On the contrary. It only means that, precisely because God works in every happening and in every moment of history, we are called to respond to his claim on us. God's operation in history should mean both consolation in difficult times and encouragement in difficult tasks.[14]

More than that, however, God's creation is like the rainbow which can be seen only when we view it from a particular place. So too creation. Creation can be experienced in its fullness when we obey God and behave as God's trustees. Belief in creation will not be effective as long as humans remain blind to God's presence in creation.

Clearly then, belief in creation has to do with the very essence of being human and meaning in life.[15] For belief in creation says that God's effective presence both in humans and in creation that enables and mediates life belongs to the very self-understanding of humans. Seen in this perspective, the biblical belief in creation has little to do with subduing the earth. Such an attitude would be a betrayal of the belief in creation. Expressed positively, this implies that because creation is part of the self-understanding of humans, they have a special responsibility towards it.

3. Responsibility for Creation

The responsibility of humans consists in listening to God's effective presence in creation and in responding to it.[16] This is not a romantic affair, but a necessary aspect of meaning in life. Creation is part of the self-understanding of humans and, therefore, humans must listen to the claims that creation makes on them

---

von der immer geltenden Totalabhängigkeit alles Seins vom Schöpfer zugleich jene bleibende Eingeborgenheit der Welt in den göttlichen Sinn, die der Glaube Vorsehung nennt."

[13] See C. Westermann, *Genesis 1-11: A Commentary* (Minneapolis: Augsburg, 1984), p. 606: "At the end as at the beginning, the world and humankind are in God's hands. God's universal action has always remained the broader perspective of his action toward his people. The Bible can only speak of the end of the world and humankind because God is the creator of them both."

[14] P. Smulders, "Schöpfung," in *Sacramentum Mundi: Theologisches Lexikon für die Praxis*, Vol. 4, p. 399: "*Gott* ist der Urheber des Alls, und zwar der personale Heilsgott, der sich als reine Liebe und Initiative geoffenbart hat."

[15] *Ibid.*, 400: "...die Schöpfungstat Gottes darf nicht als eine äußere Bedingung der geschöpflichen Eigentätigkeit gedacht werden, sondern als deren innerer Kern. Auch in meiner Tätigkeit ist Gott mir innerlicher als ich mir selbst. Der Schöpfer ist 'nicht kategoriale Ursache neben anderen in der Welt, sondern der lebendig dauernde transzendentale Grund der Eigenbewegung der Welt'."

[16] M. Heidegger's saying about the human person as the guardian of being (Hüter des Seins), appears to me to be entirely in this direction.

and respond to it.[17] In this way alone can they reach fullness of meaning in life.

The expression "claims of creation" will be understood better when we appropriate Raimon Panikkar's understanding of *Ontonomy*.[18] Ontonomy is the law of being (*nomos tou ontos*) and refers to the fact that there is a specific dynamics (= law) in every aspect of life, but in such a manner that it harmonizes with the all the other aspects of being. That is why it is not so much the categories of our thinking that are important as the ontonomic relationships of things, that is, the harmony of the pluriformic and specifically different "voices" of all created things. It is from this perspective that the thought-categories must be tested. Humankind is neither the centre nor the crown of creation, but its trustee and shepherd.

To perceive the ontonomic world-order, it is necessary to listen to the voices of creation. This is the exact opposite of the subject-object attitude, where humans as the subject study and analyze creation as if it were a mere object. Far from being an object, creation is the place where God "works" and "dwells".[19] Anyone who perceives the world without its Creator has a very one-sided viewpoint. There is no disputing the fact that the world has an object-aspect and that there is room and legitimacy for scientific activity – provided that it strives towards wholeness or is at the disposal of the concerns of wholeness.

The most important "component" of the world-reality is, therefore, the creative, pervasive presence which brings forth the world into existence. Hence it is one-sided to understand the world without its Creator.

A view like this may not sound modern enough in an age that is scientifically oriented. Though this is a specifically Christian viewpoint, we may not overlook an important element of our foundational experience of being-in-the-world on which it is built.[20] What is this foundational experience of being-in-the-world? When we are awake (= conscious) we perceive a whole world, not individual objects. In front of us lies a whole world *in which* we concentrate on this or that object.[21] Our understanding of the world is made more precise and more

---

[17] See F. Stier, *Vielleicht ist irgendwo Tag: Aufzeichnungen* (Freiburg/Heidelberg: Kerle, 1981), pp. 164 and 60: "Hörst du die Sprache: die 'Alles – spricht' – Sprache, die dunkle, die leise, der Dinge?" and "Hört ihr das Reden der Dinge? Versteht ihr die Sprache der Dinge? Hört ihr? Horcht!" (cited by Kessler, *Das Stöhnen der Natur*, p. 97).

[18] R. Panikkar, *Worship and Secular Man* (London: Darton, Longman & Todd, 1973), p. 52.

[19] In the Western-Christian tradition, the world is understood as God's workplace. From the perspective of Indian-Christian theology, however, it is understood more as God's dwellingplace. See regarding this F. X. D'Sa, "Gott: Prinzip oder Person: Gottesbegriff im Werden der indisch-christlichen Theologie," in K. Hilpert und K.-H. Ohlig, eds., *Der eine Gott in vielen Kulturen: Inkulturation und christliche Gottesvorstellung* (Zürich: Benziger, 1994), pp. 169-200.

[20] M. Heidegger, *Sein und Zeit* (Tübingen: Max Niemeyer, 1967), pp. 104 ff.

[21] See also G. Scherer, "Welt als Konvenienz," in *Gott, der Kosmos und die Freiheit: Biologie, Philosophie und Theologie im Gespräch*, pp. 15-16: "Nehmen wir, z.B. an, jemand sitze in seinem Zimmer. Er weiß, daß sich das Zimmer in einem Haus befindet. Er einnert sich an das Dorf oder die Stadt, in welcher das Haus steht. Die Stadt oder das Dorf befinden sich in einem

detailed through such concentration. It is in this way that we become more familiar with the world.

In a reflection like this one, it is important to note, firstly, that there is something in front of us that escapes our manipulation. In our foundational experience there is something that lies beyond our powers and our will. The world that is revealed in this experience is something that is "given" and not chosen by us. In the dynamics of the foundational experience something is present to which we are, as it were, handed over.[22] Humans are not their own makers. Their "being" does not lie in their hands. "Being handed over" means that there is a limit to what humans can do. They cannot do everything; they are not "perfect" beings. On their own they cannot reach their goal, their salvation, their wholeness (however one may speak of this). Irrespective of whatever they can achieve or realize, they have to face death in the end.

Secondly, "Being handed over" is part and parcel of the self-understanding of humans. Humans have to take note of this fact, especially when they think of meaning in life. This is also connected with the ethical realm, as well as the question of science and technology. On the one hand, there is the fact of "being handed over" and, on the other hand, responsibility to creation. The tricky question is this: when is human activity hybris and when is it responsible?

With regard to the limits set to humans, does this mean that they have to remain passive or actively attempt to go beyond them? We should not be led astray by our talk of "limits". We do not know where the "limits" lie? As far as acknowledging our state of "being handed over" is concerned, there should be no dispute. Opinions differ, however, when we try to ascertain where exactly limits are to be located.

To ascertain this, there is need of openness of understanding and purity of heart. Openness of understanding sees to it that humans dare to go beyond the limits of what they know and recognize. They dare to overcome existing limits. By nature, humans are always on the search – *the search for their limitlessness*.[23] Humans cannot accept the limits that constrain them. The limits that they

---

Land. Dieses gehört zu einem Erdteil. Weil er weiß, daß sein Haus sich auf der Erde befindet, ist ihm auch deutlich: Auf der Erde leben heißt unter dem Himmel sein. Damit wird deutlich: Sein Haus steht auf einem Planeten, dieser gehört zu größeren Sternensystemen, diese gehören in das Weltall. In einer solchen einfachen Meditation besinnt er sich auf eine von E. Husserl herausgeteilte Grundstruktur des menschlichen Bewußtseins. Für es ist alle besondere Realität, die wir Menschen erfahren, von einer 'Totalitätstypik umspielt'. Die kleine nahe Umwelt des Menschen erstreckt sich in den Welthorizont. Das Universum ist in ihr stets anwesend."

[22] See in relation to this H.-G. Gadamer, *Wahrheit und Method*, p. xxix: "Die Erfahrung der geschichtlichen Überlieferung reicht grundsätzlich über das hinaus, was an ihr erforschbar ist. Sie ist nicht nur in dem Sinne wahr oder unwahr, über den die historische Kritik entscheidet – sie vermittelt stets Wahrheit, an der es *teil zu gewinnen* gilt."

[23] G. Scherer, "Welt als Konvenienz," p. 19: "In den aufgezeigten Momenten des Totalitätsbezuges, des Seinsverständnisses, des Verlangens nach Sinn und der Fähigkeit des Menschen,

experience are for the time being. For, *the urge to go beyond what puts limits on them belongs to the very self-understanding of humans.*[24]

Purity of heart is something that in our times does not receive the attention it deserves. It belongs to the most important presuppositions of any human enterprise. Openness of understanding is the result of purity of heart. Whereas the former makes possible the crossing of limits, the latter enables a vision of what lies beyond the existing limits. It is not enough to cross existing limits; it is necessary to discern that which lies beyond them. Since this does not usually happen, it is not surprising that our age has to face side-effects whenever it crosses existing limits.

3.1. TECHNOLOGY OR TECHNOCRACY?

Techne, art, has now come in course of time to be understood as technology. *Techne* in the beginning did not come to be ruled by reason. Only when *techne*'s meaning changed into skill did technology come into being. With that *techne* fell under the realm of the Logos, which now has claimed it for itself completely. Today technology has reached its climax and become transformed into technocracy. That this is not just a play on words will become clear from what follows. Clearly, a basic distortion that blocks the way to real knowing has taken place.

The foundational experience of being-in-the-world reveals unambiguously that reality escapes our grasp, at least to some extent. We perceive it only partially; we cannot then reduce reality to the perceptible aspect alone. Over and above the realm of perception, there is an aspect of reality that escapes our reason(Logos)-consciousness. Human being-and-consciousness cannot be reduced merely to the reason(Logos)-consciousness, which has to do with what one experiences and expresses. In addition to this, there is the realm of the Spirit (or whatever one may call it), which is different from the realm of reason. What belongs to the realm of the Spirit is not accessible to the realm of reason. What the background is to the foreground, the realm of the Spirit is to the realm of reason. The realm of the Spirit cannot be articulated, but it makes articulation possible. It cannot be analyzed, but it makes analysis possible. It cannot be conceived, but it makes concepts possible.[25]

---

alles begrenzte Seiende zu übersteigen, zeigt sich sozusagen das Urgestein dessen, was wir Geist nennen."

[24] See H. Kessler, "Gott, der kosmische Prozeß und die Freiheit," in *Gott, der Kosmos und die Freiheit: Biologie, Philosophie und Theologie im Gespräch*, pp. 196 ff.

[25] R. Panikkar, *Rückkehr zum Mythos* (Frankfurt/M: Insel, 1985), pp. 10-11, writes similarly: "Man kann nicht direkt in die Quelle des Lichtes blicken, man wendet ihr den Rücken zu, um zu sehen – nicht das Licht, sondern diese beleuchteten Dinge. Das Licht ist unsichtbar. Ebenso ist es mit dem Mythos – der Mythos ist hier nicht der Gegenstand der Untersuchung, sondern der Ausdruck einer besonderen Form des Bewußtseins. Mythos und Weisheit gehören zusammen...."

Thus Spirit and reason are two distinct but valid aspects of human con-sciousness.[26] Technology today creates the impression that there is only the realm of reason and thus it contributes to the total neglect of the realm of the Spirit. The scientific and technological enterprise concentrates only on the realm of reason and thus encourages development only in the realm of reason. The realm of the Spirit lies fallow.

In this manner of procedure lies multiple disaster. Firstly, there is the loss of the wholeness of reality; secondly, there is the impression created that the realm of perception constitutes the whole of reality; thirdly, the realm of the Spirit is totally neglected; and, fourthly, humankind is developing in an extremely one-sided manner.

This exposes technology's lack of openness to an understanding of be-ing. Technology is built on the sciences, where the realm of perception constitutes, directly or indirectly, the centre. But the sciences can say nothing about the realm that is beyond that of perception. They behave like the proverbial frog in the well, which does not know any world other than its well. The perceptible, we have said, does not constitute reality, but only a part of it. Hence there is need of understanding and developing science and technology more holistically.

But is this feasible? True, science and technology have by their very nature to concentrate on the realm of the perceptible. But does this mean that they have to be by all means closed to the non-perceptible, or for that matter deny it? Could there be sciences and technologies that are so open to the realm of the non-perceptible that they allow themselves to be complemented and corrected by it? What we need, therefore, is a more holistic understanding of religion and technology.

3.2. RELIGION AND TECHNOLOGY

There is, both in religion and technology, an incorrect understanding of reality. Today both of them appear to be one-sided. Can today's religion reach salvation without technology? And is not technology without religion in danger of turning out to be ever more inhuman?

Religion is the search for meaning, for holistic and definitive meaning.[27]

---

[26] *Ibid.*, "Ein lebendiger Mythos läßt keine Interpretation zu, weil er keiner Vermittlung be-darf. Die Hermeutik eines Mythos ist nicht mehr der Mythos, sondern sein Logos. Der Mythos ist genau genommen der Horizont, vor dem jede Hermeneutik erst möglich wird. Der Mythos ist das, was wir stillschweigend voraussetzen, was wir nicht in Frage stellen. Er ist unbefragt, eben weil er de facto nicht als fragwürdig betrachtet wird. Der Mythos ist transparent wie das Licht, und die mythische Geschichte – Mythologumenon – ist nur die Form, das Gewand, in das der Mythos gekleidet ist, worin er sich ausdrückt und erhellt."

[27] Every religion proves its credibility precisely through wholeness. A one-sided religion would not be a genuine religion. The present age is a challenge for all religions to interpret them-

Meaning that is holistic and definitive is not different from a meaningful vision. The most important contribution of a religion is the vision that it mediates. But an authentic vision works holistically and has a touch of definitiveness.[28] Where the definitiveness is missing, wholeness too is missing, and vice versa. It is true that in the realm of humans, wholeness and definitiveness can never be achieved. Therefore, what is meant is that religion has to function in and mediate the direction of wholeness and definitiveness. That this is so is seen from the fact that where religion is authentic there is a constant correction and re-interpretation of its basic tenets – a correction and re-interpretation in the direction of wholeness and definitiveness.

It is a fact that every religion promises not only salvation (Moksha, Nirvana, etc.) but also the path to salvation. True salvation begins here and now. Whatever the manner in which a religion looks at salvation, the aspect of wholeness is always connected with that of definitive meaning. Religion cannot afford to overlook or neglect any aspect of life, whether body or love, happiness or health, food and shelter, world or environment, war or peace. The health of the body cannot be separated from the health of the soul. The body- or world-aspect of life may not be underestimated. It is the only way in which religion can have access to the world of humans. Whether it is ritual or sacrament or love of neighbour or keeping the commandments, the body- or world-aspect is indispensable for reaching salvation.

Because of the holistic and definitive character of religion, the practice of religion cannot afford to neglect the reality of life, for the practice of religion has to co-respond to the reality of life and keep in step with it. This, however, does not by any means imply that religion has to adjust itself to life. It only means that it has to take into account those areas in which and through which modern life develops and expresses itself. The development of technology today is so extensive and comprehensive that there is hardly any area which has remained untouched (untainted?) by it. Religion has to make itself felt in all these areas.

---

selves holistically. This wholeness certainly can no longer be attained by independent initiative. It requires intercultural and interreligious Dialog.

[28] Cf. H. Kessler, "Gott, der kosmische Prozeß und die Freiheit," in *Gott, der Kosmos und die Freiheit: Biologie, Philosophie und Theologie im Gespräch*, p. 196: "Intentionales Aussein auf das Ganze der Wirklichkeit, auf deren sinnhafte Kohärenz wir in jedem Akt des Erkennens und Strebens (zumeist unreflex) vorgreifen: darin gründet die religiöse Dimension unseres Bewußtseins.... Mit Schleiermacher könnte man Religiosität auch charakterisieren als 'Sinn und Geschmack fürs Unendliche', für das, was letzten Endes Bestand hat, deshalb grundlegenden Halt, letzten Gehalt (Sinn) und Erfüllung zu geben vermag und so allein unser unbedingtes Vertrauen (faith), daß dem Ganzen der Wirklichkeit eine einheits- und sinngebende ultimate reality als Urgrund und Ziel zugrunde liegt."

4. Retrieving the Wholeness of Creation

How wholeness can function is best illustrated by Raimon Panikkar's cosmo-theandric vision.[29] Reality, according to Panikkar, is constituted by three dimensions: the perceptible dimension, the perceiving dimension, and the depth-dimension.

The perceptible dimension refers to reality's realm of perception. Every thing has [to have] a perceptible dimension; it is the real meeting-point of the whole of reality. When no such dimension can be ascertained, either directly or indirectly, we have nothing, as far as we humans are concerned. The perceptible dimension could be called by different names: cosmic or earthly or material.

But the perceptible can be known only through the perceiving dimension. What is perceived is perceived because it is perceptible. Without the perceiving dimension, the perceptible cannot be the perceptible. Every thing that is connected directly or indirectly with humans is connected inextricably with the perceiving dimension.

The close connection between these two dimensions has a profound foundation. Just as there is no limit to the perceptible dimension, so too there is no limit to the perceiving dimension. In other words, both the perceptible and the perceiving dimensions have no limit. If there were a limit, neither would be what they in fact are. This limitlessness is the third dimension, the depth-dimension of reality.

The specificity of each of these dimensions is that none of them can be reduced to the others, that none of them is independent of the others and that all three of them together constitute reality. The dimensions are not part of reality; each of them is in the whole of reality and the whole of reality is in each dimension. There is a sort of *perichoresis*, a *circumincessio*, an interpenetration.

4.1. ONE-SIDEDNESS OF RELIGION AND TECHNOLOGY

Against a background like this, we have to ask whether religion and technology are really holistic, whether religion one-sidedly concentrates on the depth-dimension and technology on the perceptible dimension.

We ascertain that life today is being increasingly determined by technology. Not only are all the areas of life being influenced by it, life itself is being, as it were, technologized. The cyber-world is becoming both meeting-point and market-place, school and pleasure, medium and method. The personal computer appears to be in a position to put us in contact with the whole world.

---

[29] R. Panikkar, "Colligite Fragmenta: For an Integration of Reality," in F. A. Eigo and S. E. Fittipaldi, eds., *From Alienation to At-one-ness* (Villanova: Villanova University Press, 1977), pp. 19-132; and *Gott, Mensch und Welt: Die Drei-Einheit der Wirklichkeit*, ed. R. R. Ropers (Petersberg: Via Nova, 1999).

Accordingly, there is no doubt that technology has brought us blessings as well as disasters. Among the blessings are the possibilities that can bring unknown and distant humans in touch with one another, that all kinds of information are potentially available to all humans, that the latest news from the most distant regions reaches us in "no time," and that the treasure of human knowledge can be brought home at any time, etc.

The disastrous effects can be brought together under one heading: concentration on the cosmic dimension to the exclusion of the human and the depth-dimensions. The one-sided concentration on the cosmic dimension is the greatest weakness of today's technology. This manifests itself in the fact that it rarely takes note of its side-effects, on the one hand, and understands its [formal] object univocally, on the other. This is due to the fact that it goes about its business strictly one-sidedly, without stopping to consider its holistic aspects. The consequences are clear: one-sided development of the world in general and of life in particular.

Whether it is the political or the economic order, the market-forces, the social and medical fields, the military and the weapons' industry, the fields of traffic, construction and construction material, the demands of life-style and the environment, farming method, gene-research, etc., etc., – what matters seems to be only profit. This is determined by the speed and the quantity of production. And, obviously, the extent of the profits determines the extent of the power that one wields. Peace, justice, equal opportunities, and welfare for all – all this does not appear to be part of the discussion in which technology is interested. Size, speed, and profit – these are the interests to which technology is wedded. It shows neither attention nor interest in the claims that wholeness demands. What is worse is that technology does its business in the interest of only a few human beings. It has no place for the aged, the weak, and the helpless (among humans or animals or the environment). The greater the progress technology makes, the more inhuman its achievements seem to become as far as the poor and the helpless are concerned. These hardly enjoy the benefits of progress. Technology appears to serve only "the bold and the beautiful". Wherever this is the case, the beginning of the end of human society and a holistic world is taking place. The strength of a chain is directly proportional to its weakest link.

In its turn, religion does not show any great enthusiasm for the astonishing development of technology. Religion and technology relate to one another as oil and water. Religion does not see that the very roots of the scientific enterprise are one-sided and, therefore, from the very start militate against wholeness. That this is so is evident from the fact that the scientific methods which technology follows without reserve and on which it rests reduce the world to an objectified reality. It behaves as if there were only individual objects. It abstracts from wholeness and examines "objects".

It is precisely in the realm of wholeness that religion could contribute its mite. What is asked of religion is not that it should dictate to technology what and how it should go about its work, but that it should keep on reminding technology to give up its one-sidedness and move in the direction of wholeness.

But religion too is in danger of stressing the depth-dimension one-sidedly, at the cost of the human and cosmic dimensions. The praxis of religion today shows that it is falling prey to this danger. The other-worldliness of religion is in fact a short-circuiting of a holistic religiosity.

Religion is not an area like other areas of life. Rather, it shows the direction in which the whole of life has to move if it is interested in reaching salvation. Religion's task of proclaiming holistic meaning consists in drawing attention to the fact that the intentionality of all the areas of life is to strive for wholeness. The specificity of religion is that it draws attention to wholeness. Religion has to critique and point out whether wholeness is at work in the diverse areas of life.

4.2. WHOLENESS OF RELIGION AND TECHNOLOGY

Wholeness refers to the integration of the three dimensions of reality. Technology operates one-sidedly, because, supporting itself on reason, it reduces reality to the cosmic dimension alone. In the process, it neglects the human and depth-dimensions. Reason is its be-all and end-all. Religion operates one-sidedly, because, due to its exaggerated stress on the depth-dimension, it neglects the human and cosmic dimensions. God is its be-all and end-all.

The technology of the future cannot afford to build its house on the objectification of humans and their world. Similarly, the religion of the future too cannot afford to place God in the centre, as it were. The former must be open to the depth-dimension and the latter to the human and cosmic dimensions. The human, the cosmic, and the depth-dimensions are not "objects"; they constitute the cosmotheandric reality.[30] That is to say, there can be no humans when they are not connected with God and the world. There cannot be a world if it is not connected with God and humans. And there can be no God who is not connected with humans and their world.

Panikkar is right when he pleads for a threefold conversion: a movement beyond individualism, anthropocentrism, and dualism.[31] The justification for it lies in the following: Reason alone does not constitute the realm of the Logos; the realm of the Logos does not constitute the human; and the human does not con-

---

[30] R. Panikkar, "Philosophy as Life-Style," in A. Mercier and M. Svilar, eds., *Philosophers on Their Own Work* (Bern/Frankfurt-M: Peter Lang, 1978), p. 206: "God, Man and World are three artificially substantivized forms of the three primordial adjectives which describe Reality."

[31] R. Panikkar, "Medicine and Religion," *Inter-Culture*, 27:4 (1994), p. 11.

stitute the whole of being/reality.[32] If religion and technology are to become holistic, then they too have to tread the same path, namely, the path that leads beyond objectification, anthropocentrism, and the dualism of religion and technology. The perspective that treats the world as a collection of objects has to make place for the perspective that treats the world as creation. In creation there are no objects, only created beings. Furthermore, in such a perspective the human person would no longer place him/herself in the centre. The human is only a shepherd and overseer, not the lord of creation. In such a case, the mystery of creation would not easily be overlooked.[33]

A technology that looks upon every thing as an object cannot be at the service of human persons in the long run. Technology has to concentrate on the object-aspect of reality, but it may not reduce the world to an object. It does this whenever it stresses only human interests and neglects the interests of the cosmos and the depth-dimension.

Religion and technology are guilty of dualism, because technology stresses "this-worldliness" and religion "other-worldliness". Technology must avoid giving the impression that it can create a heaven on earth. If it does so, it becomes inhuman. Humans are not merely body; they have an aspect that goes beyond the body. A technology that either denies or ignores this aspect becomes inhuman. On the other hand, religion may not create the impression that it has nothing to do with this world. A religion which does this cannot be authentic. In such a case, it would be like salt that has lost its characteristic of saltiness. For real salt penetrates and affects the whole dough. Like salt, then, religion has to penetrate and affect the whole world.

Religion and technology are worn-out concepts today, but once they become holistic they will relate to one another as person and body, where one cannot be without the other nor can one be reduced to the other. A healthy body reveals the person and the person animates (= anima-tes). Technology that blocks the way to the depth-dimension of reality turns out to be technocracy, and religion that neglects technology is far from being holistic. The other way round, technology that shows concern for wholeness does not have to make propaganda for religion thematically and religion that mediates holistic meaning does not have to interfere with technological matters.

In other words: technology must re-discover *techne*. Only in this way will it

---

[32] R. Panikkar, "The Myth of Pluralism: The Tower of Babel – A Meditation on Non-Violence," *Cross-Currents*, 29:2 (1979), pp. 214-15.

[33] Cf. W. Blake:

> To see a World in a grain of sand
> And a Heaven in a wild flower,
> Hold Infinity in the palm of your hand
> And Eternity in an hour.

"Auguries of Innocence," in L. Untermeyer, ed., *A Treasury of Great Poems English And American*, Vol. 1: From Chaucer to Burns (New York: Simon & Schuster, 1964) (Reprint), p. 608.

be transformed into a techniculture. Religion will have to discover once again the depth-dimension in humans and their world. Only then will it be authentic and so lead to a spirituality that is relevant.

5. Gratitude and Commitment

To be a believer today implies participation in the multicoloured religious rainbow, because the search for meaning is culturally and religiously multicoloured. It is in the context of such a rainbow that one can acquire a more holistic self-understanding as a believer.

5.1. TO BE A BELIEVER IN AN AGE OF TECHNE

Creation is more than "world"; it is God's presence that is creatively at work in the world. Such a world is God's gift and where there is a gift, there is the basic attitude of gratitude. Whether we are believers or not, it is a fact that the world is a "given". The only sensible attitude toward what is "given" is gratitude. Humans in whom gratitude is missing will find it difficult to remain human.[34] Gratitude is basically not a matter of etiquette, but the culmination of being human. It is humans and not machines that can "thank" and say "thank you!" Here we have the fundamental difference between technocracy and techniculture. Technocracy works logically and without concern for its surroundings; but techniculture sees to it that it leads to gratitude. From the viewpoint of logic, gratitude has no place in the process. But humans are more than "Logos," more than "logic". Techniculture recognizes this and goes about with the surrounding world in such a way that this "more" becomes manifest. Gratitude is such a manifestation in holistic humans and their society. It is gratitude, not any payment or recognition, that urges committed humans in their depths to care for Mother Earth and all its children. For real commitment is born of gratitude.

In order to reach wholeness, it is our task to take to the path that leads from technocracy to techniculture. On such a path there has to be an interpretation of faith that clarifies and builds bridges in a world that has shrunk into a global village. For such a task we need the help of two companions on our way: a prophet and a pontiff (bridge-builder). The prophet sheds light and clarifies in the context of dialogue with neighbouring traditions what is good and bad in all

---

[34] Thankfulness should remind one of the Christian Eucharist (expression of thanks). The following passage, from the Second Vatican Council's "Decree on the Ministry and Life of Priests" (*Presbyterorum ordinis*, No. 5), which is cited by way of example, expresses the standing of the Eucharist: "The Most Blessed Eucharist contains the entire spiritual boon of the Church, that is, Christ himself, our Pasch and Living Bread.... In this light, the Eucharist shows itself as the source and the apex of the whole work of preaching the Gospel."

traditions.[35] No tradition is free of distortions and restricting elements. These can be discovered by a prophet in the light of mutual dialogue among traditions. On the other hand, there is need to discover in each tradition the lines connecting with other traditions and build bridges with them, because we all constitute one family. This is the task of the Pontiff.

Finally, whatever may be our belief-world, the fact is that air and water, and the whole world are caught up in the process of turning into poison, and that, on the one hand, a small minority lives in luxury and, on the other, millions of humans are hungry and thirsty, and that everywhere the sense of meaning seems to be becoming weaker, not stronger. This is a bad news for both technology and religion. Hence it is necessary that all people of good will and their traditions come together, not only to deepen mutual understanding, but also to retrieve wholeness. Out of such wholeness common and just action can be born; only such action can testify to the credibility of religion and the wholeness of techniculture. What is more, it alone can retrieve the unity of the human family in this world.[36]

---

[35] See M. E. Tucher, "The Role of Religions in Forming an Environmental Ethics," in D. T. Hessel, ed., *Theology for Earth Community: A Field Guide* (New York: Orbis, 1996), pp. 146 f.

[36] In its "Declaration on the Relation of the Church to Non-Christian Religions" (*Nostra aetate*, No. 1), the Second Vatican Council stated: "One is the community of all peoples, one their origin, for God made the whole human race to live over the face of the earth. One also is their final goal, God. His providence, His manifestations of goodness, His saving design extend to all men, until that time when the elect will be united in the Holy City, the city ablaze with the glory of God, where the nations will walk in His light."

HUMANKIND'S RELATIONSHIP WITH NATURE AND PARTICIPATION IN THE PROCESS OF CREATION BY TECHNOLOGY FROM AN ISLAMIC POINT OF VIEW

Asghar Ali Engineer

1. Creation, Human Beings, and Nature

According to all scriptures, it is God who created this universe and all that is within it. According to the Qur'an also, Allah is the creator of this universe, of nature, and of human beings. There is also the Darwinian theory of evolution. Some support the theory of evolution and reject what is called "creationism" and some people support the dogma of creation and totally reject the concept of evolution. The Qur'an also talks of creation; but the question is whether it rejects the concept of evolution? It is essentially the question of interpretation, after all. The most important question is: are the concepts of creation and evolution mutually exclusive? Most people would maintain yes. But I think they are not necessarily exclusive. They are rather inclusive. The question is: evolution of what? It is evolution of what exists. The Darwinian theory of evolution, if properly understood and interpreted, does not necessarily reject the idea of creation, though it was thought to have done so. In fact, rationalism was emerging in Europe with great verve in the 19th century and the rationalists were looking for explanations for the coming into existence of human beings and various other species. Darwin's observations and the theory he built on the basis of the empirical evidence he collected became a powerful weapon in the hands of rationalists. It is as if the rationalists were waiting for someone to theorise along these lines and Darwin became their hero, who provided them with the much-needed explanation.

Those people who held orthodox religious points of view rejected, on the other hand, Darwin's theory and dubbed it "atheistic" and damned it with all the force at their command. For them, belief in evolution amounted to interfering in the domain of God. The human being, according to this point of view, was a humble creature of God and his duty was to submit humbly to the Will of God. He could not interfere with the work of God, let alone aspire to be His partner. Thus creationism and evolutionism were on a collision course. They are even today for many believers. Both creationists and evolutionists took narrow and dogmatic views. In fact, creation and evolution are complimentary, rather than

47

P. Koslowski (eds), Nature and Technology in the World Religions, 47–58.
© 2001 *Kluwer Academic Publishers. Printed in the Netherlands.*

contradictory. Both of the concepts support each other, if dogmas are discarded. The theologians take a very narrow view of creation, as if creation were a one time perfect product and, as a result of God's word "be," it "became." It is this narrow understanding of the concept of creation which is quite problematic. Similarly, the rationalists, too, took a very restricted view of evolution and totally ruled out the possibility of creation. Such a view is equally problematic – evolution of what, if nothing existed before?

Thus if we talk of human partnership in the process of creation, we will have to drastically change our thinking about both creation and evolution. However, today, according to the believers, it is God and His power of creation that is final and cannot be interfered with. In this view, the human being is a mere helpless creature without any power. The opposite point of view holds the human being as supreme, God as mere myth, and evolution as the final reality. It is very difficult to reconcile such opposing and dogmatic points of view, and the question of human partnership with the divine is not posed.

Whatever the point of view, one thing is clear: The human species is an integral part of nature. Nature can exist independently of human beings, but human beings cannot without nature. The very sustenance of human beings is derived from nature. It is nature that sustains humans. Both those who believe in religion and those who do not support this point of view. Those who believe in God maintain that God created the entire universe, and at the end human beings. Those who reject religious belief also maintain that humans are products of nature. Thus, the relationship between humans and nature is, so to say, beyond dispute.

What is Islamic point of view?

What does the Qur'an says about creation and evolution? If it is interpreted literally, as it is by orthodox believers, the Qur'an also teaches the concept of creation, leaving no place for evolution. However, if literalist interpretation is replaced with metaphorical and symbolic interpretation, there can be room for reconciling the concept of creation with that of evolution. As far as creation is concerned, the Qur'an says, "And when He decrees an affair, He says to it only Be, and it is" (2:117). The orthodox theologians maintain that once whatever Allah decrees, is created by these words. But many others, especially the modern interpreters, do not agree with this understanding of the above verse. Thus Maulana Muhammad Ali, a modern commentator of the Qur'an, observes:

> *Kun fa-yakun* is the recurring phrase in which Allah's act of the creation and annihilation of things is spoken of in the Holy Qur'an. It is not meant by this that there is no gradual process in the creation of things: evolution in creation is in fact plainly spoken of in the very first words of the Qur'an, where God is spoken of as *Rabb* (Evolver) of worlds, the *Fosterer of a thing in such a manner as to*

make it attain one condition after another until it reaches its goal of completion.
It is, in fact, an answer to those who think that the creation of things by God is
dependent on the previous existence of matter and soul and the adaptability of
their attributes. The argument given here in the word *badi'* is that man, who
stands in need of matter to make things, also stands in need of a pattern after
which to make them, but God stands in need of neither. The verse seems particularly to refer here, however, to the revolution that was to be brought about by
the Prophet. It seemed an impossibility to men but Allah had decreed it. And in
fact, the revolution brought about in Arabia by the Prophet was so wonderful that
the old heaven and earth of the peninsula may be said to have been changed into
new ones.[1]

Thus it will be seen that there are many shades to the word *"kun"* ("be").
Allah's command to create human beings can certainly play a role in further
shaping things. It is for man to rise to the level both through perfection of
technology and value orientation, where he can play a role of partnership with
Allah in perfecting or re-shaping the process of creation. A noted poet of Urdu
Muhammad Iqbal says: Raise thyself to such level that Allah, before shaping
the things will consult thee what thy opinion is! Is human partnership in divine
creation possible and desirable? Can the modern technology support the process
of creation? Well there are differing points of view. Some maintain that human
beings, since they are themselves created, cannot become partners in creation or
participate in the process of creation. The other point of view accepts such a
possibility. In every religious tradition, be it Christian, Hindu, or Muslim, there
is no single point of view. The orthodox viewpoint always differs from the liberal and progressive one.

Before we deal with this question, we would like to throw light on the concept of creation in the Islamic scripture, i.e. the Qur'an. The Qur'an uses two
terms for creation: *ibda'* and *khalaqa*. Both have distinct meanings. *Bada'* refers to creation out of nothingness. Such an act of creation does not require any
imitation of others and anything so created is called *badi'*. Allah is called
mubdi', who creates without any pre-existing material or without any tools or
without space and time. Such an act of creation is only for Allah; no one can
assist him or participate with him in this process of creation.[2]

Khalaqa, on the other hand, also means to create; but it has a different shade
of meaning. It means creation with tools, with assistance, with pre-existing material and in time and space. When it refers to Allah, however, *khaqlaqa* could
be synonymous with *ibda'*, i.e. creation without any assistance, without any
tools or outside time and space. Thus Allah has created this universe, the heav-

---

[1] Maulana Muhammad Ali, *The Holy Qur'an*, 6th Ed. (Lahore: AAII Publishers, 1973), p. 51-
52, f.n. 163.
[2] Cf. Imam Raghib, *Mufradat al-Qur'an.* Urdu trans. Sheikhul Hadith Maulana Muhammad
Abdahu (Lahore: Ahle Hadith Academy, 1971), p. 76.

ens and earth, and for that the Qur'an uses both *bada'* (2:117) and *khalaqa* (3:16). But as for humans, the term *bada'* cannot be used, because human beings cannot create without assistance, without tools and outside time and space.[3] Thus no human being can participate, as far as Allah's creation in the first sense is concerned, i.e. human beings cannot be *badi'*, but they can be *khaliq*. It is in this sense that the Qur'an describes Allah as *ahsan al-khaliqin*, i.e. best of the creators (14:23).

Thus, in the later sense, human beings are also creators and can become participants in the process of creation. Here it will be important to point out that creation cannot be isolated from sustenance, and that sustenance is not possible without deep concern (compassion) for the creation. Allah is, therefore, described in the Qur'an not only as creator but also as sustainer (*rabb*) and as *Rahman* (1:2-3). Allah creates this universe, sustains it, and feels deeply concerned for His creation. Human beings thus also participate in the process of creation by participating in the process of sustenance and caring for the creation of Allah. To preserve and protect this earth, which we inhabit and which is the creation of Allah, and to feel deeply concerned for it is very important for us humans. Allah has taken upon Himself to be Merciful and Compassionate. The Qur'an says, "He has ordained mercy on Himself" (6:12). Thus, He cannot but be Merciful. Mercy is His very nature. It is this nature of God that sustains the universe. Thus, human participation in sustenance of this universe – this earth as far as human beings are concerned – is participation in the process of creation. Human beings have to design technology to further the process of sustenance of this earth.

As pointed out above, human beings cannot create out of nothing, only out of existing material and with the help of tools. And modern technology is the most powerful tool that human beings have designed. However, since technology is a tool, not an end in itself, it has to be such as to strengthen the sustenance of human beings on this earth and the earth itself. Modern technology can be destructive as well as creative. The question is: is our technology such as to enable us to participate in the process of creation and sustenance? Or is it otherwise? There is no categorical answer, because there is much ambiguity in human action. There is no such ambiguity in Allah's action, as He has ordained mercy on Himself. Among His names in the Qur'an we find *Nur* (light), *Rahim* (Merciful), *al-Hadi* (The Guide), *al-Wahhab* (Generous who gives in plenty), *al-Razzaq* (Provider and Sustainer), etc. All of these names are Allah's attributes, which indicate how He looks after His creation and how He is the Benefactor of His creation. But for Him the creation would not survive.

This is not true, however, as far as human beings are concerned, even though they aspire to be participants in the process of creation. Allah creates and sends

---

[3] Ibid, p. 316.

His guides for human beings to guide them to enhance the value of His creation. However, human beings give greater importance to their selfish interests than to the creation of Allah. He even devises utterly destructive technology to promote his selfish ends. He has created nuclear technology in order to destroy God's creation? Nuclear technology not only wreaks havoc and destroys all that is here on earth, but also destructively affects future generations of human beings, plants, water resources, etc. through radiation. Yet human beings, despite being fully aware of the destructive nature of nuclear technology, do not desist from creating it. Not only that, but several countries have nuclear weapons which together can destroy this earth several times over and also destroy all future possibilities of creation of life for millions of years.

For human beings to participate in the process of creation with God, they have to devise technologies which will be life enhancing, not life destroying. To accomplish this, human beings must rise above selfish interests and imbibe positive values contained in the Divine Attributes. As I wrote above, human actions are, unlike God, ambiguous and capable of both enhancing and destroying life. It can be said that Allah also destroys life, in the sense that He ordains death – the death of all species. This destruction, however, is not for the sake of destruction, but for fresh creation. Human destruction, on the other hand, is not only for the purpose of destruction, but also for destroying all possibilities of life to come into existence. Allah in His Mercy has gifted humankind with the precious gift of intellect, which has tremendous life-enhancing, creative potential. This potential can be actualised only when humans rise above selfish interests and devise technologies that can help humanity to flourish.

Intellect is not only a precious divine gift, but also a powerful tool of human creation. As pointed out above, divine creation does not depend on any external tool, whereas human creation does. But God Himself has gifted humankind with the power of reason, so that it can assist Him in the process of creation. Thus it becomes the sacred duty of humankind to make the best possible use of intellect and to become a part of the divine process of creation. It is in fact Allah's will that humankind assists Him in the process of creation by preserving His creation through devising appropriate technology. That is why the Qur'an says, "We created human being in the best make." (95:4). This implies that human beings are endowed with all the positive qualities, physical as well as mental, corresponding to the functions that this particular creature is meant to perform. It is for man to make the best possible use of these innate qualities given by God. But the next verse also describes his innate evil tendencies, when it says, "Then We render him the lowest of the low." (95:5). A similar statement is made in verse 91:7-8: "He reveals to it (i.e. human soul) its way of evil and its way of good."

Thus human beings have potentialities for good as well as for evil in them. It is for them to decide – and human beings are free agents in this sense – whether they want evil or good to prevail. This evil and good is also reflected in the technology that human beings devise. Human beings as such in this sense can either be divine agents or agents of Satan. Adam was created – as we read in both the Bible and the Qur'an – and given freedom to eat the fruit of all trees freely, except of the one which was forbidden to him. However, Adam was tempted by his desire to eat the fruit of the forbidden tree, and was expelled from the paradise. The children of Adam also feel tempted again and again to test the fruit of this forbidden tree and thus miss out on the paradise of peace and positive creativity again and again and have to live with destruction, violence, and conflict.

Human intellect, through invoking divine guidance, knows what is good and what is bad, and yet often opts for what is evil. Human intellect is capable of great creative feats that enhance the quality of life on earth. And, in fact, today human intellect has performed these feats of creativity and devised technologies that are life enhancing. We can refer here to the production of several life-saving drugs through modern research and technology. Also the technologies available for many intricate surgical operations, which were simply unthinkable half a century ago, have certainly enhanced the lifespan of human beings and also the quality of life. But, and this is important to note, these technologies are not available to all human beings. Because the distribution of income is highly skewed, the poor cannot avail of these technological feats. Today despite these miraculous technologies, thousands die in the Third World even for want of simple medicines. The Divine Compassion would not admit of it. As pointed out above, the Qur'an describes Allah as the Sustainer of the whole universe, of which all human beings are an integral part. In the eyes of Allah, all human lives have equal value and hence all need to be sustained equally, without any discrimination. Thus, the creation of technology is not sufficient for participating in the divine process of creation and sustenance. It is also necessary that it be equitably available to all. It can be equitably available only if wealth is not concentrated in the hands of a few and all facilities and life-enhancing amenities are made available to all. It is, then, no wonder that the Qur'an stresses the equitable distribution of wealth and strongly condemns its concentration. Thus, the Qur'an says, "And those who hoard up gold and silver and spend it not in Allah's way – announce to them a painful chastisement" (9:34). Again in 59:7 the Book warns that the riches should not circulate among the rich only.

It is necessary to point this out, because the modern technology – be it in the field of health or information or any other field –through which human beings participate in enhancing the quality of divine creation and enrich it, is too expensive and unaffordable for millions of people in developing countries. In fact, these people find it difficult to sustain themselves. Even basic health services are not available to them, let alone the latest technology of surgery, transplantation of organs – especially the transplantation of hearts and kidneys. Today these techniques developed by human beings are highly useful in saving lives and aiding the divine act of sustenance. Though these surgical and transplantation technologies are saving a large number of lives and thus enriching the divine act of creation, still much larger numbers of human beings are far from able to afford them. To create a technology to participate in the divine act of creation is one thing; more importantly, to make it available to all those needing it is something else. Both aspects are equally necessary.

2. Cloning and Transplantation

Of late there has been breath-taking progress in technologies of creation of life, apart from adding to its sustenance or its enrichment. One can mention here the technology of cloning. Animal clones have already been produced. Dolly the baby sheep was cloned very successfully by scientists in Britain. Not only that, but Dolly gave birth to three lambs. According to a news report

> Dolly gave birth to two males and one female lamb.... "We are delighted", said Dr. Harry Griffin, assistant director of the Roslin Institute near Edinburgh. It was a second pregnancy for Dolly, who gave birth to a single lamb, Bonnie, last spring. All four lambs have the same father, a Welsh mountain ram named David.[4]

According to the report: "'Dolly and her lambs are in good health. The births were unassisted and all three are suckling well', the Institute announced." The birth of Bonnie almost exactly twelve months ago confirmed that despite Dolly's unusual origins, she is able to breed normally and produce healthy offspring. The birth of these three lambs is a further demonstration of this, the institute said. Dolly herself was born in the institute in July 1996 after scientists cloned her from a cell from another sheep's udder. She was named after the singer Dolly Parton. Her creators say it is important to breed from cloned animals to check for any unexpected changes in their offspring.[5]

It was not surprising then that the scientists began working on human cloning also. According to the *Daily Mail*, dated 17th June 1999, scientists in the United States have cloned the first human embryos. Using methods similar to those which produced Dolly, the cloned sheep, they produced a male embryo comprising nearly 400 cells, the British tabloid said. The scientists at Massachusetts-based Advanced Cell Technology, Inc. then incinerated the embryo after two days. They wanted to produce human body tissue, which can be used to treat patients with various conditions, including nerve damage, diabetes, and

---

[4] See *The Times of India*, Bombay Edition, 3 April 1999.
[5] *Ibid.*

Parkinson's disease. A DNA-loaded nucleus of a human cell was extracted from a skin sample from a man's leg and then inserted into the outer protein of a hollowed-out cow's egg under laboratory conditions, said the *Daily Mail*. The egg was then placed in a laboratory dish and soaked in a chemical solution, which fooled it into thinking it was a newly-conceived embryo. The cells then reportedly began to develop into an embryo.[6]

These breath-taking technologies have made humankind a real participant in the process of creation. It is no longer a mere possibility, but a hard reality. But another important question remains, which is of an ethical and religious nature. Should cloning be permitted? It may not be highly objectionable ethically as long as cloning is confined to animals alone. But when it comes to human cloning, serious ethical issues arise. Should it be permitted at all? Some are making serious objections to animal cloning itself, as it paves the way for human cloning. A Saudi Islamic theologian objected to any form of cloning, dubbing it as interference in God's domain. He even went to the extent of saying that scientists who are engaged in this research should be given exemplary punishment. Of course, this can be dismissed as an extreme view. But the ethical question remains and cannot be dismissed out of hand.

Even transplantation of organs such as kidneys has been greatly misused, especially in poverty-stricken societies like India's. Not only do poor people sell their kidneys to rich patients, but they are often deceived by Mafiosi, who perform operations on false pretexts to remove such vital organs and sell them to needy rich patients and make huge profits. Many such cases have been reported in the press. Of course, legislation has also been enacted, but it is not sufficient to check such malpractice.

Corruption and malpractice, however, cannot be cited as reasons for prohibiting the transplantation of organs. Organ transplants have saved the lives of many human beings. But still there is no unanimity among Islamic theologians on the issue. Some still think the transplantation of organs amounts to *muthla* (mutilation of a divinely-created human body) which is strictly prohibited by the Prophet of Islam. Others, however, argue that it does not amount to mutilation of a human body, as organs are not cut from it out of hostility or disrespect, but only to save another human life.

These theologians who do not oppose transplantation of human organs, however, invoke the doctrine of what is called in Islamic *shari'ah* the doctrine of *darurah*, i.e. necessity. They argue that the Holy Qur'an even allows eating of pork if a human is dying of hunger and no other food is available. So, if a human being is dying and needs transplantation of a kidney or heart, it could be extracted from another human person, provided his life is not endangered or the donor is already dead. Also, they opine that what is *haram* (prohibited) in

---

[6] *The Times of India,* 18 June 1999.

shari`ah should not be used for transplantation. For example, the heart of a pig should not be used for transplantation in the body of a dying Muslim. Many liberal Muslim Indian theologians have discussed these issues at length and compiled their discussions into a volume.[7] There are many Muslim patients who refuse to accept the transplantation of organs until permitted by an authentic religious authority. These *fatwas* (religious edicts) compiled into this volume are highly useful to save the lives of such Muslim patients.

Cloning, needless to say, is much more controversial than mere transplantation of organs. According to orthodox Muslim theologians, it amounts not only to *muthla* (mutilation of a human body), but also amounts to directly assuming the function of a Divine Creator, which cannot be permitted at all. This is a theological objection. But an ethical objection must also be taken into account. Can human cloning be ethically permitted. Is whatever is technologically possible also ethically permissible? This is a most important and fundamental question, which needs to be answered satisfactorily. Even scientists and other secular authorities, let alone the theologians, differ on the ethics of cloning.

Thus Patrick Dixon, author of *Futurewise* (Harper Collins, 1998), said in an interview:

> Making cloned babies has real dangers. Terrible mutations could result as well as huge emotional risks to the child. What will it do to a cloned son to look at his dad and see his twin brother, his mother and see his sister-in-law? The cloned daughter knows that she will have impacted wisdom teeth on her 15th birthday, she'll be gray at 40 and suspects her mother is giving her music lessons to prove how talented her own genes are. And there are serious risks of abuse by weirdos and the powerful.... Many people in America are deeply uneasy about deliberately creating an identical twin embryo of an existing person with the express purpose of destroying it for use of its tissues. As a doctor, I know we need gene technology to feed the world and cure disease. But we don't need human cloning.[8]

Michael Shermer, a publisher of *Skeptic* magazine, on the other hand, advocates human cloning and sees no harm in it. Opposing any ban on human cloning, Shermer writes:

> This Promethean theme of limiting knowledge is a common one not only in science fiction, but in science fact. For every mythic Icarus who flew too close to the sun, there are real-life scientists who got their wings clipped for daring to push their frontiers too far. Birth control? Only God can do that. Life extension?

---

[7] Maulana Mujahidul Islam Qasmi, *Zarurat-o-Hajat* (Delhi: Islamic Fiqh Academy, India, 1995).

[8] Patrick Dixon, "The Brave New World of Human Cloning: Animals Are One Thing, Humans Are quite Another," *Times of India*, Bombay Edition, 12 January 1999.

Only God can do that. Euthanasia? Only God can do that. We should not be surprised, then, that when a British government advisory commission encouraged the legalisation of research into cloning human tissues and organs for therapeutic uses, it was met with opposition from both religious and secular groups. Cloning? Only God can do that....

Shermer further writes:

Nonsense! Most of us are alive because of medical technologies and social hygiene practices that have doubled the average life span in this century. What's godly or natural about heart-lung transplants, triple-bypass surgeries, vaccinations or radiation treatment? What is godly or natural about birth control and birth enhancement technologies? Absolutely nothing. Yet we cheerfully accept these advances because we have grown accustomed to them and, more important, we have benefited from them. I propose that we lift the ban on all research into cloning – including humans. My hypothesis is that nothing evil will befall society. Most of the horror laden scenarios proposed by moralists are already addressed by the law; a clone, like a twin, is a human being, and you cannot harvest the issues or organs of a twin.[9]

3. The Islamic Point of View

Thus it will be seen that the ethical aspect of technologies like cloning remains highly controversial. Even secularists differ, let alone the religious authorities. It is a well know fact that in America many conservative Christians are highly opposed to abortion, and the pro-life and pro-choice debate is highly emotional. These new medical technologies, even if they immensely benefit human beings and increase their chances of survival, remain unacceptable to many on "ethical" grounds. They not only consider it as undue interference in God's domain, but also immoral.

The Islamic point of view has never been unanimous. There is no concept of church in Islam and no one authority can issue a religious edict and expect it to be accepted universally by all Muslims. Muslims are not only divided into numerous sects and schools of jurisprudence, but also into liberals and conservatives. Thus there cannot be any unanimity on these questions also. Of course, so far human cloning has not been seriously debated in the Islamic world. In fact, this question has not been raised in Islamic countries so far, as it is still not conversant with it. But the more common view would be that it is interference in Allah's work.

---

[9] Michael Shermer "Go Ahead and Clone; It Is just another Tool of Science," *Times of India*, Bombay Edition, 12 January 1999.

If one goes by the Qur'anic spirit, however, the technology of cloning should not be rejected outright. The Qur'an invites believers to reflect deeply on Allah's creation and, in fact, those who so reflect are indulging in an act of worship – *'ibadah*. The Qur'an repeatedly invites believers to reflect deeply about oneself and how the universe has been created. Thus the Qur'an says, "Do they not reflect within themselves? Allah did not create the heavens and the earth and what is between them but with truth, and (for) an appointed term" (30:8). Yet in another verse it says: "Those who remember Allah standing and sitting and (lying) on their sides, and reflect on the creation of the heavens and the earth: Our Lord, Thou has not created this in vain! Glory be to Thee!" (3:190)

These verses equate deep reflection on the creation of the universe and all that is in it with worship. Thus this act of reflection on creation is very significant. It is this attitude which creates a scientific mind that explores the mysteries of creation and tries to participate in the process. Such an act of reflection on God's creation does not in any way challenge His authority, as some orthodox theologians maintain, but rather reinforces His authority. It is such reflection that makes human beings appreciate the intricacies of divine creation, and motivates them to devise technologies to try to either recreate them or make them survive longer through these technologies. Today, scientists are trying to map the chromosomes and understand the intricacies of DNA, genes, etc. It is through study of these basics of life that various possibilities, including prolonging life or bringing extinct animals to life have arisen. Now DNA science can even enable scientists rebuild the dead dodo.

According to one report, scientists are to extract DNA from a dodo for the first time, raising the prospect that the animal whose name is synonymous with extinction could be resurrected. The British experts will recover fragments of genetic material from a preserved head and foot kept in Oxford University's Museum of Natural History. The research will identify the closest living relative and may pave the way for the species to be resurrected one day.[10] These technologies, similarly, will enable scientists to modify and improve the quality of human life. Thus, according to the British astrophysicist Stephen Hawking, the advent of new and improved kind of "genetically modified" human beings will be inevitable in the centuries to come.[11] Again, such possibilities are not devoid of ethical controversies. Any technology, for that matter, can be misused, as pointed out earlier. However, the use or misuse can be, to some extent, controlled by suitable legislation. Again, it is these technologies which have made it possible to prolong human life. It is said that the children born today will be able to live to 130 because of medical advances. For the first time, scientists have quantified the extra years that breakthroughs in human genetics, organ

---

[10] See *Times of India*, Bombay Edition, 30 March 1999.
[11] See *Asian Age*, Bombay Edition, 14 March 1999.

cloning, and the biology of ageing will add to people's lifespans. They believe that by 2050, scientific advances will be adding 50 years to the current average age of 75 for men and 79 for women, precipitating radical changes in the way people live, plan their careers, spend their leisure time, and raise their families.[12]

4. Conclusion

Modern technologies, it will be seen from the above discussion, have tremendously increased the human potential for participating in divine creation. Today humankind is trying to understand not only human biology, but also the remotest galaxies, stars, and planets hundreds of light years away. As the noted theoretical physicist Michio Kaku of the City University of New York put it, "We are making the transition from discerning the laws of nature to becoming masters of it." In other words, scientists are trying to play God and this potential is going to increase tremendously in the new millennium.

No religion, much less Islam, opposes this. Islam invites human beings again and again to master the understanding of the nature of divine creation. It is only the 'Ulama, (those in possession of knowledge), the Qur'an says, who can better appreciate the great power of divine creation and it is these 'Ulama from amongst the servants of Allah who really fear Allah, because they know what the Divine Power is! (35:28). Only the 'Ulama can really have a sense of humility, because they know the vastness of divine creation. And it is these 'Ulama who, being in possession of the knowledge of creation, can devise technologies to participate in creative activities. Participation that improves the quality of creation is quite praiseworthy, since the human being is also a divine creation, and a being graced with the most precious gift of intellect can become an instrument of improvement of the quality of life on this earth, if not in the entire universe. Deeper reflection upon life, on one hand, and upon the vastness of the universe, on the other, makes him really humble and enables him to fear God in the real sense. Thus, by studying the universe and the process of life on earth, the human being fulfils the most important duty Allah has charged him with. Participation in the process of creation through these humanly devised technologies to improve the quality and span of life is a real act of worshipping God.

---

[12] See *Times of India*, Bombay Edition, 16 February 1999.

DISCUSSION OF THE RELATIONSHIP TO NATURE AND TECHNOLOGY IN JUDAISM, CHRISTIANITY, AND ISLAM

Presentations:

MICHA BRUMLIK: Humankind's Relationship with Nature
                           and Participation in the Process of
                           Creation through Technology in the
                           View of Judaism

FRANCIS X. D'SA: The World as Creation and Creation as a
                           Cosmotheandric Reality in Christianity

ASGHAR ALI ENGINEER: Humankind's Relationship with Nature
                           and Participation in the Process of
                           Creation by Technology from an Islamic
                           Point of View

Moderator: PETER KOSLOWSKI

Summary: FRIEDRICH HERMANNI

1. Creation and Freedom

The Jewish religion does indeed assume that the world was created by God, but it nevertheless believes that human beings are free to act both rightly and wrongly. Thus, the idea of a Creator God does not imply determinism in Judaism. How is the relationship between freedom and creation seen in Indian Christianity? (BRUMLIK)

In the Indian tradition, it is not the question of human freedom that stands in the foreground, but the problem of blindness to reality (*maya*). In so far as human beings in their blindness reduce the reality of the world to an object, they are not free and are led by false interests. Therefore, in the Indian tradition, the ultimate goal of the human person is liberation from this blindness and the false interests that result from it (*mokṣa*). *Mokṣa* can succeed only through a self-opening to the secret of the world. In addition to the perceptible and the perceiving dimensions, this deep dimension must be recognized as the third dimension of reality. The "purity of heart" that contains the overcoming of false interests is the condition for such a vision of what goes beyond the boundaries of percep-

P. Koslowski (eds), Nature and Technology in the World Religions, 59–63.
© 2001 *Kluwer Academic Publishers. Printed in the Netherlands.*

tion. It is also the opening of the self to the deep dimension that is understood as wholeness. But since human beings are in fact never disinterested, it is difficult to describe them as free. (D'SA)

2. The Abrahamic Religions, Creation, and Nature

There exists the thesis that the Abrahamic tradition, to which the three speakers belong, was conducive to the development of technology, because the relation of God to the world is interpreted as an act of making. Is there such a specific inclination of the Abrahamic tradition toward technology? Or are the differences between the three religions so large that we cannot talk about it in this respect as *one* tradition? (KOSLOWSKI)

What is called control of nature today has been shaped more by the development of modern man than by the Abrahamic tradition. Modern man essentially changed the biblical tradition in the fifteenth and sixteenth centuries and broke from the ancient-Christian and ancient-Jewish understanding of the world. The early-modern development of autonomous subjectivity is the sufficient prerequisite for the control of nature.

Concerning the concept of "making," there is an important difference between understanding the creation of the world as a metaphor for the completion of a workpiece and interpreting it as a master's linguistic act. If creation is the completion of a workpiece, we can speak of a subject-object relationship. If the world was created through language, we cannot. (BRUMLIK)

BRUMLIK is correct in saying that the modern development of technology is to be attributed to modern thought, not to a biblical tradition. The question of the extent to which this thought can be separated from its roots, however, remains open. (D'SA)

Talking about the Abrahamic religions appears to conceal more than it clarifies. Concepts such as *maya* and *moksa*, which are of importance in Indian Christianity, have nothing to do with what can be called Abrahamic. (BRUMLIK)

Moksa seems to designate an extremely individual spiritual event. The Qur'an, on the contrary, attaches special importance to the community of believers. (ENGINEER)

Although there are many similarities in these three religions, in view of the fact that one cannot even speak of a unified Islam, one can hardly speak of *the* Abrahamic religions. (ENGINEER)

Is the concept of "making" really at the center of discussions of a Creator God? The question is much more what it means today to believe in such a God, and, therefore, is a hermeneutical question. Furthermore, a statement about the creation is not a rational proposition, but a dogmatic proposition, and must be treated as such. (D'SA)

3. The Bible and the Relationship between Humans and Nature

To what extent do other passages in the Bible, such as Genesis 1,28 ("Fill the earth and subdue it") play a role for the relationship between humans and nature and the human understanding of technology? (KOSLOWSKI)

The prophetic texts and the Book of Proverbs can be referred to as possible sources. It can be derived from the prophetic texts that nature also suffers under human injustice. This can be seen already in the utopias and visions of Isaiah's peace with animals. Although the creation is fundamentally good, it can be true that, as a consequence of human injustice, it lives non-peacefully and is not redeemed. This state of not being redeemed, however, is not fundamental, but only a consequence of unjust human actions. In the Book of Proverbs it is written that nature itself is pervaded by reason and for its part can teach humans the principles according to which they should live. (BRUMLIK)

4. The Relationship between Humans and Nature in Hinduism

Are there stronger approaches to a careful relationship with nature in the Hindu tradition than in the Christian tradition? (KOSLOWSKI)

In the Hindu tradition the human self-understanding is interpreted differently, and, therefore, the relationship of humans to nature is also different. Humans and nature cannot be separated from one another as they are in the biblical religions. Thus the human body is also regarded as a part of the cosmic being. (D'SA)

5. Human Cloning, Mind and Body, God and the World

Where in the individual religions are the greatest problem zones of technology seen? (KOSLOWSKI)

Human cloning clearly crosses a limit for Jewish ethics. Making a new human being and, therefore, the renunciation of the way of reproduction prescribed in Genesis contradicts God's will. Since at the moment it cannot be known to what extent cloning serves the saving of life, it cannot be legitimated by this highest principle of Jewish bioethics. (BRUMLIK)

Cloning is not creation from nothing – only God is in a position to do that – but creation from something and, therefore, from something that was in turn created by God. The human person uses materials and intelligence that are given by God. Anything that the human mind creates only shows God's creativity. It is too early to reach a verdict about cloning. Every kind of technology can be misused. The question is: *For what purpose* is technology used, not whether cloning is intrinsically morally good or bad. Only the objective toward which technology is employed is ethically relevant. (ENGINEER)

Catholicism teaches that God creates every individual soul from nothing. Only the body is created by the act of procreation, not the soul. From that it would follow either that we cannot possibly clone human beings or, if it is possible, that we must reconsider the Catholic teaching. (KOSLOWSKI)

A splitting of mind and body in this sense does not originate from the Bible, but instead from the Platonic tradition. The Bible thinks much more integrally here. (BRUMLIK)

Cloning, along with many other technological developments, is a result of a certain world view, in which the world is reduced to an object. This objectification can be understood as original sin. Since the world is more than an object, however, the separation of humankind and the world reveals a false understanding of this world. Such an attitude is unacceptable for a religious person. This is also true of the separation of God and the world, as it takes place in the Abrahamic religions. (D'SA)

R. BALASUBRAMANIAN emphasized in the First Discourse of the World Religions that a distinction between Brahman ("World Soul," God) can be found increasingly today even in Indian thought. (KOSLOWSKI)

Brahman and the world cannot be separated from one another, in so far as the inspired person is described in the *Bhagavad-Gita* as the person who discovers his own being in the being of everything. The individual indeed has limits, but the person can be enlarged by entering into relationships with other persons. (D'SA)

A precise distinction between God and world seems, however, to be a step forward. The Abrahamic religions place a great amount of emphasis on the statement that God is *not* the world. (KOSLOWSKI)

In the Vedānta there is a clear distinction, but no separation, between God and the world. "I am not different from God," understood in Christian terms, does not mean "I am God," but "I am God's." (D'SA)

6. Technology, Human Persons, God

D'SA had emphasized that technological progress has not benefited the poor and the elderly. This fact appears, however, to be more of a problem of politics than one of technology itself. (Remark from the audience)

The effects of technology are *actually* directed against the poor. Therefore, the question must be asked whether the development and use of this kind of technology is not a fundamental mistake. Is it possible to conceive of a kind of technology that functions comprehensively? (D'SA)

The concept of a comprehensive species of technology is a contradiction in itself, since technology is based on a subject-object relationship. The comprehensive use of technology appears, on the contrary, to be possible. (BRUMLIK)

In the developing nations, not everyone has access to technology? That is based on an economic problem. Precisely the poor, however, could profit from a new kind of technology. (ALBRECHT)

It is unambiguous that the biblical world view is open to anthropocentrism. How can we overcome this anthropocentrism? (question from HORUZHY to D'SA)

The anthropocentric interpretation of the Bible is not established by the Bible itself. The Bible is more comprehensive than it appears to its interpreters. (D'SA)

The Bible describes God and his actions as anthropocentric. The very concept of action is anthropocentric, since nature does not act. Consequently, an acting God has characteristics of a person. If one were to remove this concept of action from God, the entire concept "God" would break apart, since a God that does not act is not God. (BRUMLIK)

In Islam there are two species of conceptions of God. The "Hanbalites" advocate the thesis that God's essence remains inaccessible and that it is impossible to speak about God. The theologian al-Ash'arí, for example, defends the opposing position that a certain analogy between God and the world exists and, consequently, that concrete statements about him can be made. (ENGINEER)

D'SA said in his presentation that the human person is more than Logos. We read in John 1,1, however, that Christ is Logos and nothing more than Logos. Is the human person more than Christ? Such a restricted – postmodern – understanding would not be a Christian position. (HORUZHY)

The contemporary use of "Logos" is characterized by a rational understanding. If we were to return to the original meaning of the concept, this would be correct. (D'SA)

In response to a question from the audience, about whether suffering from technocracy is a necessary phase, through which God lets man attain a new discovery of himself, BRUMLIK answered that the technologizing of the world does indeed give humans new ways to become aware of their creatureliness, but that God surely does not intervene in history in this way.

THE PROCESS OF THE DEIFICATION OF THE HUMAN PERSON AND TECHNOLOGY IN EASTERN-ORTHODOX CHRISTIANITY

Sergey S. Horuzhy

> now the machines demand
> their celebration.
>
> Source of our weakness
> now, and in vengeful rage
> ruining our heritage,
>
> us shall these things at length,
> us, who supply their strength,
> serve in all meekness.
>
> R. M. Rilke, *Sonnets to Orpheus*, I, XVIII
> (trans. by J.B.Leishman)

1. The Christian Universe: Man, Nature, and Process

Christianity is not a religion of the Cosmos, but the religion of the Person. This classical statement about the subject and type of the Christian religion states nothing directly about the status and role of the human person in the empirical world: the subject of the religion is God as Person, and the notion of Divine Person (Hypostasis) surely does not coincide with any empirical mortal individual. Nevertheless, the personalist character of the religion implies immediately quite a number of cardinal anthropological principles. Already the Old Testament states that man is created "in the image and after the likeness" of God (Gen 1,26); that man is placed to have supremacy over all the world beings (Gen 1,28); that he enters into a special personal relationship with God, "makes a covenant" with God. The anthropological situation is outlined here quite precisely:

P. Koslowski (eds), Nature and Technology in the World Religions, 64–80.

1) Man forms an ontological unity with the world, as a "creature", a created being, who is as such and as a whole separated by an ontological distance and split from uncreated, Divine being;

2) Although man is united with the world, he is singled out in it, holds the central and leading position in it, and has power over it, given by God;

3) Although man is separated from God, he keeps a constant and mutual, spiritual and existential connection with Him, and this connection of God and man is a decisive factor in the destiny of all the world and creation.

It is obvious here that the biblical worldview is completely anthropocentric.

The New Testament, which states that it is the "fulfillment" of the Old, develops and complements these biblical positions, sometimes radically. The event of the Incarnation, i.e. the union of the Divine and human natures in the Person of Christ, probably brings the element of anthropocentrism to the limit; but in no way does it deny or destroy the ontological unity of man with the entire creation. As an *ontological* event, it relates to the destiny of the entire creation, and man stands out in it as a "representative" of created being, "the sum and concise summary of World", to use the formula by Father Pavel Florensky. These features of Christian anthropocentrism should be taken into account when we discuss the critique of anthropocentric views that is quite popular today. The critique states that anthropocentrism means the egoistic subjugation and exploitation of the environment by man, it belittles Nature and is deaf to its life and beauty, it generates dangerous strategies that threaten the global balance – and it is time to reject it. But, in fact, this critique is valid only for certain versions of anthropocentrism and it embraces neither the general concept nor its Christian form. Anthropocentrism as such is the principle of "centrality" (essential, dynamic, or teleological) of man in the world, and this principle does not determine the type of man's relationship with other parts or elements of the world; it is compatible with the attitude of service to, as well as domination over, these parts. As for Christian anthropocentrism, it combines the singling out of man with the statement of common destiny of the entire creation and this combination actually amounts to the attitude of *man's responsibility* for this common destiny. What is more, one should keep in mind that anthropocentrism is in a certain sense not an option but an immanent predicate of man's situation. As demonstrated by phenomenology, man is always placed within the horizon of his lived experience as a subject; he is "in the subject perspective". Hence in any *Weltbild* built up by man, the world is that of the subject's lived experience, or the "World-as-Experience"; and only after taking this properly into account can one try to build up some discourse "in the perspective of the Other". *Mutatis mutandis*, this is valid for the global aspect as well, i.e. for the experience of

mankind as a whole. And all this means that what we need now is not the de-
clarative rejection of anthropocentrism, but its new and profound rethinking, fit
to the present conditions.

The anthropocentrism of the Christian world-view is combined with the
theocentrism and Christocentrism of the view of being, the integral reality of
God and World; and it is theocentrism and Christocentrism that emerge as the
leading and preponderant principles of the Christian outlook. In the treatise "De
Opificio Hominis", St. Gregory of Nyssa disputes the significance of the ancient
principle, calling the correspondence of Man and World Microcosmos and Macrocosmos. He says that the meaning of the nature of man is revealed in the relation of man, not to the world, but to God:

> The pagans say that man is a Microcosmos, composed of the same elements as
> the Universe. But ... what is the importance, if we consider man as an image and
> likeness of the world? The greatness of man does not lie in his likeness to the
> created world, but in his being in the image of the Creator's nature.[1]

The totality of being is determined by the ontological axis God – Man. The
relation of man to God is most rich, dynamic, and dramatic; but the scene of its
unfolding is, in the first turn, the inner reality of man, his spiritual and emotional world. Hence the relations Man – Cosmos and Man – Nature turn out to
be ontologically secondary and less important in the drama of being; and so for
many centuries they stayed far in the periphery of Christian beliefs. Both the
theoretical problems of these relations and their practical development were
almost completely the prerogative of the secularised sphere of science, technology, and economy.

In our age, however, under the influence of many factors at once the situation changes profoundly. Below we shall discuss these factors in detail, as they
belong to basic features of the modern anthropological situation and technological development. Now we only mention one of their results: the problems of
the relations of man with nature and the situation of man in the Universe reveal
more and more profound religious aspects, and Christian thought brings them
more and more into its orbit. Its approach to this circle of problems is based on
principles that were present in the Christian outlook for a long time. But today
they come to the foreground, are comprehended anew and given new spheres of
application. We shall concentrate on three such principles or key properties of
the Christian world-view, according to which this world-view is:

1) anthropocentric
2) dynamic and processual
3) energetic

---

[1] St. Gregory of Nyssa, *On the Constitution of Man* (St. Petersburg, 1996), p. 50 (in Russian).

These three principles have different bases in the tradition: as we noted, the anthropocentrism is akin to the Judeo-Christian Tradition as a whole; the dynamic and processual view of the world is characteristic of Christianity and, to a much lesser degree, of Judaism; and finally, the energism, grasping of the reality of man and world "in the dimension of energy", as a system of all kinds of impulses, drives, activities, etc., is deeply rooted in the all-Christian vision, but is explicitly expressed chiefly in the Eastern Christian Tradition, Orthodoxy.

Although the remark by St. Gregory of Nyssa reduces the importance of the idea of man as the Microcosmos for Christianity, by no means is this idea completely excluded from Christian anthropology. In fact, it conveys the message of Christian anthropocentrism quite adequately, but only after being profoundly reassessed and generalized. As the Microcosmos, man is not a part, but the centre, collecting focus and Nexus, principle of connectedness of created being. From this point of view, the idea appears as a structural paradigm and ontological principle. In the first function, it is the assertion of the isomorphism, structural identity of Micro- and Macrocosmos; in the second one, it is the ontological identification of the modes of man's being and created being as such (similar to the identification of man's being and "being-there", *Dasein*, in the "fundamental ontology" of Heidegger). Hence it follows that the fulfillment of the destination of created being is achieved, in the first turn, in man, through man and by man.

As for the dynamic aspects of the constitution of man and the world, the key feature of the Christian dynamism is that it refers, first of all, not to physical, but to metaphysical (ontological) dynamics, that of being (*das Sein*) and not essent (*das Seiende*). Always, unconditionally, for Christianity being is a process; but only because of this and depending on this the world is also a process; the dynamics of the world is determined by that of being (there is here a common element with Hegelianism). However, the type and character of the World Process do not follow from the properties of the Ontological Process, as they are stated in the Christian kerygma, in any direct or evident way. That is why the dynamic and processual character of the Christian world-view is not evident and indisputable. In the most influential and widespread versions of this world-view in the West, this character was neglected and sometimes even denied openly. In his well-known study of modern global problems, Ervin Laszlo writes:

All attempts thus far to bring the biblical tradition into accordance with the permanently evolving reality have been ineffective. Although the majority of Judeo-Christian religions possess historical perspectives when they deal with the spirit-

ual development of a person, they lose this perspective when they deal with the
evolution of mankind.[2]

This is a very dubious statement. Besides the unfounded application of the
evolutionary paradigm to the World Process as a whole, the author completely
disregards the ontological dynamism of Christianity emphasized above. In fact,
already the biblical mythologems of Creation and Fall in their classical patristic
treatment imply the dynamic and processual character of the world's mode of
being or, in the discourse of human sciences, the historicity of this mode. The
act of Creation provides the world with the beginning, determines its mode of
being as a "begun being", but it does not determine the ontological status and
ontological situation of the creature completely. This status remains open, since
the question about the end still remains open: a priori, created being, having the
beginning, can possess as well as not possess the end. In other words, two different modes of created being are possible, namely, the creature, respectively,
possessing and not possessing the predicate of finiteness. (In the theological
discourse, these two modes are, respectively, fallen and unfallen, perfect (Mt
5,48) created being). Making bifurcation one of the central notions of his picture of reality, Laszlo does not notice that the biblical ontology of Creation is
the classical and, in fact, paradigmatic example of ontological bifurcation: the
actual created being necessarily presupposes the choice between the two possible modes, and the mythologem of the Fall, or Original Sin, is nothing but the
act of this choice (made in favour of the mode of finiteness).

In the Christian ontology, however, the chain of ontological events is not yet
concluded with the Fall, the choice of finiteness and mortality. The event of
Christ is stated by the kerygma as a direct continuation of the drama of being,
bringing into it a new element of dynamism: that is why it is considered to be a
"new beginning" and Christ "the second Adam". The death of Christ on the
cross is, according to the kerygma, "the redeeming sacrifice", the necessary and
sufficient ontological pre-condition of Salvation. And salvation is here nothing
but the overcoming of the fallen state (by means of unifying with Christ), the
fundamental predicates of which are sinfulness and mortality; in ontological
terms, it is the ontological transformation, leaving or transcending the mode of
finiteness for the other of the two modes of created being. (In the theological
discourse, the human nature of Christ belongs precisely to the perfect created
being, and due to that the unification with Christ is not the self-realisation of the
fallen created nature of man, but its transcendence.) But Salvation is in no way
a predetermined necessity! The Saviour does not surmount man's sinfulness and
fallenness instead of man himself. He creates for man the situation in which

---

[2] E. Laszlo, *The Age of Bifurcation: Understanding the Changing World* (Amsterdam, 1991).
This is a translation of the Russian translation (Moscow: Put', 1995, No. 7, p. 97) back into
English.

they are surmountable. The event of Christ does not constitute (in the sense of phenomenology) a completely pre-determined process, but once more, like the First Beginning, the Creation, ontological bifurcation: the creature will either remain in the mode of finiteness or transcend this mode.

Such an assessment of the event of Christ as the initiation and beginning of a new, bifurcational, and transcending dynamics of created being is characteristic especially of Eastern-Orthodox Christianity. Here a dynamic picture of being emerges, in which the *deification* (θείωσις, *deificatio*), actual transformation of the nature of man into Divine nature, comes out as the central concept. This concept was brought up already by the early Church Fathers of the second century (cf. Irenaeus of Lyon, *Adv. Haer.* III.X.2), then it was expressed by the famous formula by St. Athanasius of Alexandria: "God became man, so that man would become God" (*De Incarn.* 54); but for Western theology it always remained marginal and somewhat ambiguous. In the Eastern-Christian discourse, on the contrary, it was developed into a key concept, conveying man's ontological destination; so that the whole drama of being, or Theocosmic process, is represented as a single whole, the ordered series of inseparable ontological events: Creation – Fall – Incarnation – Deification.

2. Creation, Fall, Incarnation, Deification

Here deification is the extra-worldly, meta-empirical goal or telos of created being, which is achieved by means of a process of a special kind, carrying out an actual ontological transformation. Thus, created being is represented as the dynamics of deification; but it has to be stressed that it is *ontological* dynamics, of which the empirical contents is not yet revealed by its initial theological and ontological definitions.

As a postulate of faith, the theological and philosophical thesis of deification is, undoubtedly, holistic and global: it tells about the destiny of created being as a whole, all the spatial-temporal Universe or Macrocosmos. However, cardinal features of the Christian discourse, its personalist character (in the theme of God) and anthropocentric character (in the theme of World), unavoidably brought the effect that deification was also related to the destiny of the individual, the created person, in which case it was the meta-anthropological telos of a specific anthropological strategy. Realisation of this strategy, or anthropological process, ascending to deification, is the sense and subject of the Orthodox school of spiritual (mystico-ascetic) practice, the *hesychasm*. Hesychast practice, cultivated in Orthodoxy from the fourth century until the present day, has been developed into a refined holistic practice of the Self, in which, based on a special technique of "incessant prayer", a successive stepwise process of the auto-transformation of man, directed towards deification, is built up. This ancient tradition, typologically related to Eastern schools of spiritual practice, is recognized as the true core of Orthodox spirituality. Evidently, it represents a radically dynamic treatment of man; however, this dynamism hardly touches upon the relation of man to society, nature, or the Cosmos. In contrast to the relation to God and to oneself, one's own inner world, these relations turn out to be secondary and marginal, precisely as noticed above.

It should not be otherwise, however, in the sphere of ascesis: by its very essence, the spiritual practice in its classical forms is a *sui generis* anthropological laboratory, where, on the microcosmic scale, in the material of an individual human existence, one discovers and develops the dynamics of ontological transformation of present being, which is, in the case of *hesychasm*, the dynamics of the ascension to deification. At the same time, as stated above, the principle of deification as such should be conceived as a global principle, relating to the Macrocosmos. Hence, if only the Christian world-view accepts the principle of the isomorphism of the Microcosmos and Macrocosmos, we conclude that the dynamics of the ascension to deification, found in the ascetic experience, should be interpreted on a universal plan: as a dynamical paradigm or model, which in some generalized form also determines global dynamics, that of the World Process. The Christian anthropocentrism comes out here in the dynamic aspect: *the anthropological dynamics of spiritual practice should serve at the same time as a core and paradigm of global dynamics*; in other words, the dynamics of deification on the global plan is built up on the basis and by the pattern of a certain anthropological core, which is provided by the dynamics of spiritual practice. This is an essential conclusion. First, it means the inversion of the basic relations in the vision of reality, corresponding to impersonalist religions and theories: in this vision, the anthropological reality does not determine the global dynamics of the Macrocosmos, but, on the contrary, is determined by this dynamics, as by the "laws of nature". Second, it provides some initial insights into the sense and role of technology in the vision of the reality, determined by the principle of deification: obviously, in this vision the designing and technical activity directed to nature and Cosmos is needed in order to exteriorize and globalize the dynamics of the spiritual practice, turning the latter into the paradigm of the dynamics of the Macrocosmos. As a result, strategies of the "inner" and "outer" activity of man should converge; combining and merging with each other, they should become two components of a unified ontological dynamics, following the same paradigm.

The dynamics of deification, on the anthropological as well as global plan, is singled out by a number of specific features; in particular, as noted above, it has the bifurcational and transcending character. These features are both closely related to one more important characteristic, which we have called above the *energetic* character of the Christian – and chiefly Eastern-Christian – vision of man, the world, and being. Usually and predominantly, European theology and metaphysics are developed in the essentialist discourse, as a discourse about essences and categories, going back directly to them, like ideas, forms, laws, etc. This way is almost unavoidable for discursive and abstract thought, which unfolds itself by means of constructing notions and syllogisms. Eastern-Christian thought was moved, however, in the first turn, not by intellectual tasks, but by the practical goal of achieving a certain special kind of experience, namely, communion with God in union with Christ. In this case, the central part belonged to the phenomenology of human energies, i.e. all kinds of impulses, somatic, psychic, and intellectual, movements of thought, will, emotions.... Man was represented here by his projection into the dimension of energy, or "being-action", in ontological terms, and appeared as an energetic formation, system of heterogeneous and interrelated energies. And the goal was to bring this system, or the "energetic image" of man, to such form, in which all the energies of a human being are oriented, in harmonious and coordinated unity, towards deification. The latter is also treated as an energetic concept, namely, the union of all man's energies with Divine energy, or grace. Thus, what is necessary for deification is the collaboration and coordination, "coherence", of all man's energies with Divine energy (though the physical term is applicable in a quite limited degree, since the interaction of energies is here not a physical, but spiritual act, personal communion of God and man). This common, harmonious, and unified organization of the two ontologically different energies is described by the Byzantine theological notion *synergy* (συνέργεια).

The achievement of synergy and deification (conceived energetically) is exactly the content of hesychast practice. The process of advancement to the meta-anthropological telos of deification is thus the successive stepwise transformation of the energetic image of man, building up a series of anthropological energetic structures, or "energoforms", ascending hierarchically to energoforms, corresponding to synergy and deification. But, as soon as deification is not only the telos of the spiritual practice, but also a dynamic and global concept, the anthropological strategy of the energetic ascent can be interpreted at the same time as a prototype, pattern of global dynamics. On the global plan, the deification comes out as the meta-historical telos of the global dynamics, as on the anthropological plan it is the meta-anthropological telos of spiritual practice. This globalising interpretation of the anthropological dynamics of deification, rooted in Christian anthropocentrism and Eastern-Christian energism, is what we describe below.

The global process, implementing the energetic ascending dynamics, is not just a cosmic and natural process; it also has an ontological and super-natural dimension, as a process in being and not only in essent (*das Seiende*). In this ontological dimension, it presents a rather close parallel to a certain type of natural process. When the world, as an energetic formation, directs itself (its energies) to an extra-worldly telos that implements a different mode of being, it represents an "open system" in (the totality of) being, similar to physical open systems, which are open in the horizon of empirical being. An important property of physical open systems is that they can have an external source of energy. Next, a special class of open systems is formed by systems in states far from equilibrium. If such a system possesses an outer source of energy, the flux of this outer energy through the system may generate a progressing process of structuring. These specific processes are studied in a new branch of physics, the synergetics, and it was found that they have numerous parallels in social and biological systems.

Now the analogy with the ontological dynamics is quite clear. The dynamics of deification, on the anthropological as well as cosmic plan, is the dynamics of an open system, for which Divine energy comes out as the "ontologically external source of energy". Since the substance of this dynamics is the generation of a hierarchy of energetic structures, synergetic processes provide the closest parallel to it. Some of these processes, e.g., those of the classical chaos, present quite graphic, structural similarity to the ontological dynamics, since their substance is also the generation of an ordered series of dynamic structures. Thus the etymology does not lie, and indeed synergy has much to do with synergetics. This conclusion is of heuristic value for anthropology, disclosing dynamic and system-theoretic meaning of many stages and features of spiritual practice. Let us give one example. The synergetic parallel tells us: if a process takes the form of spontaneous generation of a hierarchy of dynamic structures, the system in question should be first brought to a state, removed far from the equilibrium, from all the region of stable regimes. It means that the dynamics of deification, both in the form of spiritual practice and on the global level, should have a certain anthropological analogue of the "state far from the equilibrium" as its starting phase. Such starting phenomena for spiritual practice are religious conversion and repentance (μετάνοια) and hence our parallel provides their synergetic interpretation, showing them as "removed far from the equilibrium" or border regimes of consciousness and the whole human being.

Thus, in addition to social and biological applications, we discover religious and anthropological parallels to synergetic processes; and one can say that the first discovery of such processes was made centuries ago in the hesychast ascesis. However, the dynamics of deification has unavoidably capital distinctions from natural processes. As an ontological transformation, it is not unfolding and actualisation of the available human nature, but its transcendence; and it also has defining features of personal and dialogical communion. Hence it follows that it is not an evolutionary or deterministic process or a process of the organic type, in which the development of some "seeds" or actualization of some form given beforehand takes place. At the same time, it is not stochastic dynamics devoid of any ordering or orientation.

Like the anthropological strategy of spiritual practice, the global dynamics of deification is not at all a single possibility, which is to be realized with necessity. On the contrary, its realization is most difficult and problematic, because it demands the conscious decision and concentrated effort, complicated organization and coordination of all levels of global hierarchical systems. The topology of reality is always of the bifurcation type, admitting plurality of the development scenarios. This means that, besides the dynamics of deification, other types of global dynamics are possible; and one can describe them using the same methodological paradigm, which considers global strategies as exteriorizations (universalizations, extrapolations, etc.) of anthropological strategies. This anthropocentric approach (which can be interpreted as a certain enhancement of the anthropic principle in cosmology) becomes more and more justified in our age, as the phenomenon of man becomes increasingly important as a global factor.

In our anthropological model,[3] we introduce the basic concept of *Anthropological Border*, which is the sphere of limiting phenomena of human experience, where the leading characteristics and predicates of human existence in its normal empirical forms start changing. Following the classical philosophical method of defining an object by means of characterizing its border, we define man in the dimension of energy as the "ensemble of strategies, oriented to the Anthropological Border". Spiritual practice is the only one of such strategies that is oriented to the actual ontological transformation or, synonymously, to the ontological Anthropological Border. As for other "Border strategies", they stay within the horizon of present being, which means that they are oriented to other parts of the Anthropological Border, where the latter is not ontological, but only "ontic" (in Heidegger's sense, i.e. relating to essent and not to being). We have found two kinds of them: virtual strategies, oriented to the transition to virtual reality, and strategies induced from the Unconscious, which are studied in psychoanalytic phenomena, such as neuroses, phobias, complexes, etc. Similar to spiritual practice, both of these kinds also admit generalized interpretation as universal dynamical paradigms, applicable to social and other macrosystems in anthropocentric models of reality. (One can remember in this connection that Freud himself considered it necessary to study global generalizations of the patterns of the Unconscious, or "pathologies of cultural communities", such as "neuroses of civilizations", "phobias of epochs", etc.) As a result, in the same way that our anthropological model is determined by the complete topic of the Anthropological Border, including all three kinds of Border strategies, so the ensemble of global generalizations of the Border strategies determines a model of global dynamics in the anthropocentric paradigm.

---

[3] S. S. Horuzhy, "On the Anthropological Model for the Third Millennium", *Vestnik RGNF* (1999), No. 3 (in Russian).

3. Global Dynamics of Deification and Technological Factors

Let us now turn to the role which the phenomena of technology should play in the outlined model of global dynamics. Interpretations of and approaches to these phenomena are countless, but the anthropocentric character of our model suggests that in order to include them into its orbit we have to rely on the *anthropological interpretation*, developed by A. Gehlen, supported by many authors and treating all kinds of technology and technological activity as certain manifestations of man. Here technology is "the ability, inherent to man, to change nature in accordance with his goals.... This ability of man is inborn, has its origin in the nature of the consciousness and represents one of natural human potencies".[4] The anthropocentric attitude is implemented in our model in the form of the structural and dynamical isomorphism of the Microcosmos and Macrocosmos; and one of the basic conceptions of technology, following the anthropological interpretation of the latter, is fairly in accordance with this form. This is the known conception of the "projection of organs" (*Organprojektion*), according to which all technological tools (engines, instruments, devices...) in their essence and nature are man-made "projections" (substitutes, prolongations, amplifications...) of various organs of the human body; as well as the opposite, bodily organs are "organic prototypes" of technical tools. Rudiments of this idea could be found in philosophy long ago. Theories that stated the teleological and purposeful character of the world quite often illustrated this purposefulness with the correspondence "organs – tools" (Maimonides, 13th century, Bossuet, 18th century, et al.); on a more abstract level, Hegel treats man's activity as his exteriorization, projecting oneself out-there; etc. But in the explicit form, both the conception and the term "*Organprojektion*" have been presented in "Philosophie der Technik" by E. Kapp (1877). In Russian philosophy the idea was actively defended and developed by P. Florensky (1882-1937) in the book *By the Watersheds of Thought* (1917-22, publ. 1990).

The idea of the projection of organs is rather concrete, and its substantiation consisted mostly in the demonstration of correspondences between concrete technological tools and bodily organs. For instance, the hand and the palm, with their variegated functions, provide the prototype for all the multitude of tools, instruments, machines of the seizing, pressing, squeezing, etc. principle; the system of limbs and joints is the prototype of all devices with hinges, pulleys, levers, etc.; the nervous system has direct correspondence to electric nets; the eye is projected on optical and photographic technique; finally, the projection of the body as a whole is the house and other architectural edifices. Such an angle of view is no less adequate to the modern technological development; comput-

---

[4] H. Beck, *Philosophie der Technik: Perspektiven zu Technik – Menschheit – Zukunft* (Trier: Spee, 1969), p. 42.

ers and the Internet embody the projection of the human brain not an inch less directly and graphically than the shovel embodies the projection of the hand. But, nevertheless, for taking into account all topical aspects of the problem of technique, some modernization of the idea would be needed. It was noted, e.g., that today it should be complemented with the "analysis of the back action and influence, which new artificial organs had and will have on further development of man".[5] As demonstrated by countless facts, new organs do not preserve the natural proportions of the human being, and, instead of serving man, they frequently harm him, sometimes on a catastrophic scale. In addition, the idea in its present form takes the social aspects of technique into account poorly: it is important that "new organs" frequently are not only created owing to certain social factors, but can be used only collectively; so that they belong not to individuals, but to communities, and produce new connections and new social fabric.

For us, however, different aspects are important. It is essential that technology, understood as the projection of organs, appears as a direct practical realization of the structural and dynamic identity of the Micro- and Macrocosmos: all the sphere of reality technologically assimilated by man in its operational structure, and hence also in its dynamics, implied by this structure, turns out to be organized "in the image and after the likeness of man", in the anthropological paradigm. As a result, the isomorphism itself can be reinterpreted: in a new context, it is not a theological or philosophical postulate, as well as not a given empirical fact, but a created characteristic of reality, the result of technical activity of man in the world. Hence it follows a certain methodological approach to problems of global dynamics and human strategy in Nature and the Cosmos. According to the described anthropocentric attitude, strategies of man in Nature in their essence and character are nothing but the projection of some energetic features (functions, properties, predicates...) of anthropological reality; whence the Macrocosmos (the sphere of assimilated reality) in the dimension of energy, structurally and dynamically, is basically, *grosso modo,* similar to Microcosmos. Anthropological strategy turns out to be the key to global dynamics, and problems of global development by means of the projection principle go back to anthropological problems and features of the anthropological situation.

The immediate implications of this are twofold, concerning, first, the principles of the appraisal of present trends of global development and, second, the basic principles of the considered type of global dynamics, namely, the global dynamics of deification. In the first case, we try to interpret the modern global problems, negative trends, and phenomena as reflections of problems and trends of the anthropological situation: we discern here projections of diseases, vices, and weaknesses of man, stigmata of his finiteness, in philosophical terms, or

---

[5] H. Sachsse, *Anthropologie der Technik: Ein Beitrag zur Stellung des Menschen in der Welt* (Braunschweig, 1978), p. 424.

fallenness, in theological terms. One usually ranks among the cardinal problems of the technogene civilization of the present day the uncontrollable development and growth of the technosphere, ecological problems (pollution of the environment, exhaustion of natural resources, destruction of natural ecosystems, etc.) and also bioethical problems, brought forth by the progress of medical and biological technologies (euthanasia, cloning, transplantation, transformation of the existing and creation of new biological species, etc.). Anthropological roots can be easily discerned in all of these problems.

Christian ascetic anthropology characterizes a wide spectrum of negative phenomena in the structures of personality and behaviour of man by means of the concept of *passion* (πάθος). In the framework of the energetic vision of man (see Part I above), the passion is defined as an "unnatural" organization of the energetic configuration of man, a special kind of this configuration, in which all energies are subordinate to one of them, the "dominant", and form a stable structure, supporting and protecting this subordination. Thus, in contrast to usual, or "natural" configurations, which are unstable and change quickly, the state of the subordination to a dominant, or the "passionate state", has the cyclic and self-reproducing character, kindred to cyclic states of consciousness in psychiatry and cyclic trajectories of dynamic systems. In this interpretation,[6] passion is a general anthropological phenomenon, going far outside the circle of the simplest examples, like greed, lust, envy, etc., with which the ancient ascesis chiefly dealt, and close to the patterns of the Unconscious (see above). The classical ancient analysis of passions can be developed and generalized in many directions, of which two are especially interesting for our subject. First, with the development and change of the society, environment, structure of occupations, etc., the repertoire of passions is changing too. New kinds of passions emerge, among which the states with dominants related to intellectual and technical activities prevail. Second, according to our anthropocentric principle, passionate states are being projected onto the Macrocosmos, as global and collective phenomena.

Hence it is clear what interpretation is given to negative trends and phenomena of technological development in our model. Uncontrollable growth of the technosphere and its gaining of autonomy mean that the goals and values of technological development have taken the dominant position in the configuration of energies of certain human communities or even humanity as a whole. The total absorption of these communities in technical progress and slavish subjugation to it took place, and it means, in its turn, that the passionate state of a new kind, collective and global, has been formed. In this connection, it is important that in the ascesis an entire sophisticated discipline of dealing with the passionate states has long existed, including methods of discerning them at

---

[6] Cf. S. S. Horuzhy, *To the Phenomenology of Ascesis* (Moscow, 1998). (in Russian)

early stages, practices of destroying and leaving them, etc. Hence, besides providing a certain interpretation of the phenomena of uncontrollable technical development, the anthropocentric approach may also suggest some strategies of mastering them. Similar possibilities are opened by this approach in the field of ecological problems. For the most part, the latter can also be treated, basing on the generalized conception of passions; and what is more, in many cases, like problems of the destruction of the environment or exhausting resources, the anthropological roots can be traced not to some new passions, but to the oldest passions of human consumerism, like waste or greed.

As for mastering these problems, its general principles are clear enough from the viewpoint of our global model. The Universe is represented as a Mega-system, comprising the three big spheres, *Humankind – Technology – Nature*. Each of these possesses its own structure and dynamics, and equally each of these possesses some trends, potentialities of expansion, domination and suppression of other spheres, in which trends the majority of the global problems of our age is rooted. The position of Christian anthropocentrism does not at all mean that the trends of the human domination over Nature should be given unrestricted freedom. It means that the mission of man is to serve as an intelligent linking and centering agent in the Mega-system, which coordinates and harmonizes relations of all the three spheres and opens for their ensemble the prospect and possibility of the ontological transcendence. The way to this goal is *dynamic convergence*, i.e. the coordination and rapprochement of the developmental trends, dynamical regimes, and patterns of the three spheres (so that, for instance, the technological sphere should become more and more adapted and brought nearer to the patterns of Man and Nature, which process gradually develops already, together with the development of the opposite trends). This principle characterizes every stage of the globalized ascending process as a coherent unity of energies of the three spheres. Demanding the careful monitoring of all the expansion processes, it also implies a definite position in the well-known problem of the "limits of growth".

In bioethical problems we find somewhat different anthropological roots. Behind almost all of these problems, whether cloning, euthanasia, or transplantation of organs, the same conceptual and logical situation can be discerned. In all of this sphere, there exists the supreme ethical principle and value, subject to unconditional protection and preservation: and this is the human personality. The source of the problems is that in certain spheres of human activity some practices and research fields emerge, which, in some opinions, contradict the stated principle and present the threat of the destruction of personality, while, in other opinions, they do not contradict this principle and are ethically sound and admissible. The indisputable element in the situation is that the disputed kinds of activity, such as genetic engineering, have reached the practical ability of the technical manipulation of the human personality, man as a biological and intellectual being: the ability of transforming, reducing, possibly even doubling the latter. Hence the necessity emerged to introduce some protecting rules and formulate the conditions and criteria of the preservation of personality, its undestroyed wholeness. But all the attempts to do this on a satisfactory level fail. All proposed restrictions and criteria turn out to be in some or other respect arbitrary and questionable, and the consensus is never achieved.

From the viewpoint of Christian anthropology this failure is explainable. The only possible base for a universal and correct solution of the discussed problems, devoid of all arbitrariness, could be a self-consistent conception of the *(self-)identity of man*, including the definition of this notion and a sufficient set of criteria, which outline borders of the personality in its principal dimensions and are suitable for practical applications. But such a conception is not available today. The (self-)identity of man presents a profound problem, the complete solution of which is of no avail in any of the existing philosophical or psychological schools. For Christian anthropology this absence of a solution has a profound reason: the correct solution simply does not exist, since *the created individual does not possess complete self-identity*. Such completeness demands a definite ontological status and completed constitution (for which reason it is possessed either by a thing or by personality in the strongest sense of Divine Hypostasis). But the created individual is an intermediate kind of being, possessing only a rudiment or seed of the true being and personality (Hypostasis); he has only a chance to acquire a full-fledged ontological status by the bifurcational ontological dynamics of freedom, in which a certain meta-anthropological perspective is realized. It is symptomatic that the same conclusion about the absence of the truly self-identical individual was drawn on a completely different basis in the postmodernist discourse, where it was expressed by the famous formula "death of the subject". Hence we conclude that the solution of the whole complex of bioethical problems should be based on a certain solution to the problem of the self-identity of man, and this latter solution is available only in the enlarged context, namely, with the choice of a certain meta-anthropological perspective and strategy. As a result, this complex can, in principle, obtain an adequate treatment in the framework of the global dynamics of deification.

The place and tasks of technology in the constitution of this dynamics are clearly implied by its general principles. In our anthropocentric model, global dynamics is a projection of anthropological dynamics, and the global dynamics of deification is the projection of the spiritual practice in its hesychast form; so that technology should serve as a practical apparatus of this specific projecting. Hence it follows that we need to single out the principal features of the hierarchy of anthropological energetic configurations, ascending to the meta-anthropological telos, and then try to find which technologies would be able to perform the global projection of these features. The task seems to be quite concrete, but getting down to it, we discover a problem of principle, related to the very possibility of the realization of the global dynamics of deification.

Indeed, the spiritual practice, as well as each of its stages, is an energetic concept, a certain paradigm of the organization of human energies and activities; and this paradigm is, generally speaking, total, in the sense that its realization absorbs man totally, demanding the participation of all his energies. This is a classical and long-known property of mystico-ascetic practice: being immersed into it, a man "rejects the world", disconnects himself from all usual occupations of the external life. But it is the same man who should realize the global projection of this practice! As a result, one discovers in the constitution of the global dynamics of deification a contradiction or *aporia*, which can be called the *aporia* of the (in)compatibility of *Homo mysticus* and *Homo faber*. As we see it, the practical solution of this *aporia*, reconciliation of the two opposite anthropological paradigms, extreme introvert and extreme extravert, is to become one of the key anthropological problems of the future. Our preliminary analysis of it[7] shows that the solution is possible, in principle, but it demands far-going development of the resources of human consciousness, its abilities of self-observation, self-control, and coordinated combination of many activities at the same time.

Spiritual practice is holistic, and it is not just the consciousness, but the whole composition of man that changes in it. The changes are oriented to properties of the telos, the ontological horizon of the personal being-communion, which is characterized in theological discourse as the dynamic reciprocal relation of Three Consubstantial Hypostases. In its turn, this dynamic (i.e. energetic) relation is characterized as Love and its constructive correlate, the Byzantine concept "*perichoresis*" (περιχωρῆσις, *circumincessio*), meaning "going roundabout", incessant mutual exchange of being, complete giving of one's own being to the other, complete mutual acceptance and openness. Hence it follows that the being-communion, constituted in the paradigm of the *perichoresis*, is a kind of being characterized by total dynamic connection and transparence. As testified also by the mystical experience of higher stages of spiritual ascension, these two properties belong to the main predicates acquired by the anthropological reality in the ascension to the meta-anthropological telos. Accordingly, the technological aspect of the global dynamics of deification consists in achieving these properties at the global level. It is a many-dimensional and many-sided process, concrete forms of which still belong mainly to science-fiction today. For this reason, we restrict ourselves to a few remarks.

Being directed to synergy and creating in the synergetic (in both meanings, the physical and the metaphysical) the transparence and connection of the Macrocosmos, the global dynamics of deification should lead to the convergence of

---

[7] S. S. Horuzhy, *On Things Old and New* (St. Petersburg, 2000). (in Russian)

the inner and outer, anthropological and technological branches of the dynamics, and to their gradual unification. This means that it also leads to the change of the character of interaction between man and the outside world, so that the borders between man and his environment become changeable and conditional. When, with the ascension to the meta-anthropological telos, all the levels of the human being, somatic, psychic, and intellectual, are transformed, the relation of man to Nature and Cosmos unavoidably undergoes profound changes, too. All mystical traditions testify in complete agreement that in the highest stages of spiritual practice perceptive modalities of man take a radically new form. In the limit, this form has the character of so-called *synaisthesis* (συναίσθησις: the term of the neoplatonic mysticism), the unified pan-perception, belonging not to an isolated organ, but to all the transfigured human being, made transparent for Divine energies. In the hesychasm this transfigured perception has been called "intellectual senses". Hence technology in the global dynamics of deification should realize the global projection of this new perception, transforming the Macrocosmos into the scene of the cosmic *synaisthesis*, perceptive medium, which equally perceives and is open to perception, transparent.[8] Besides other distinctions, the "intellectual senses" correspond to a different form of temporality, which is specific to mystical experience (see note 7 above). And in the global projecting, which is to be realized by the technosphere, this mystical temporality of the anthropological dynamics should meet other specific forms of temporality, those of relativistic cosmological models. Touching upon the fundamental predicate of finiteness of the present being, such phenomena already enter the eschatological discourse. The dynamics of deification cannot avoid this discourse; but, as is said in Scripture, our vision of the "last things" in this life will always remain vague, as "through a glass darkly".

---

[8] Here the ideas of the global dynamics of deification have something in common with cosmic and anthropological utopias of the Russian avant-garde of the 1920s. In a similar way, there were some common motives with this avant-garde discourse in the late work by Father Pavel Florensky, where a kind of Christian global model (the model of "pneumatosphere") has been outlined. However, this model by Florensky did not follow the paradigm of deification, but that of sacralization. The relations of these two paradigms are discussed in *On Things Old and New* (see note 7).

DISCUSSION OF THE DEIFICATION OF THE HUMAN PERSON AND THE ROLE OF TECHNOLOGY IN EASTERN-ORTHODOX CHRISTIANITY

Presentation:

SERGEY S. HORUZHY: The Process of the Deification of the Human Person and Technology in Eastern-Orthodox Christianity

Moderator: PETER KOSLOWSKI

Summary: FRIEDRICH HERMANNI

1. Deification of the Human Person

In response to a question from BRUMLIK about how "deification" is to be understood, HORUZHY answered that this is an idea of the Eastern Orthodox discourse and must be understood as the perfect connection of all human energies with the divine energy. The divine energy indeed comes from another mode of being, another ontological horizon, but is nevertheless present in the human horizon. This is the theological definition and it is amplified by a physical parallel: The human person must put himself in a particular state in order to attain contact with the external energy of God. This contact between the ontological energies is called "synergy."

Energy is quantitative; deification is qualitative. Is it not problematic to apply a concept from physics to a qualitative, personal concept? (KOSLOWSKI)

"Energy" is a key concept of the Orthodox discourse and does not mean only what it means in physics. The concept was introduced by Aristotle as a metaphysical concept, and was developed further in Neo-Platonism, for example in the *Enneads* of Plotinus. The meaning of the term in the Eastern Orthodox discourse of spiritual praxis is a modification of Aristotle's understanding. The meaning of energy becomes concrete in the most important aspect: the relationship between energy and essence. Heidegger followed the Greek tradition and saw energy and essence as a unity. Energy was interpreted differently in Christian ontology. Here energy can be considered to be free of essence. (HORUZHY)

Hegel asked in *The Phenomenology of Spirit* when man will become God,

P. Koslowski (eds), Nature and Technology in the World Religions, 81–82.
© 2001 *Kluwer Academic Publishers. Printed in the Netherlands.*

and answered: When man has captivated the world under his ideational design. From that, for Hegel, the self-consciousness of God results in man through man. This kind of deification is thus an intellectual process, by which the human person subjugates himself to nature. (Comment from the audience)

For Hegel reason is the divine principle of the human person. In Christianity this deification is not only intellectual, but also corporal. Therefore, Christianity possesses a comprehensive concept and does not restrict it to the intellect. In the fourteenth century there was a dispute over this question, since people who argued philosophically could not accept that all human beings could become connected to God. (HORUZHY)

The human person is described in the Qur'an as "closely connected to God." He should reflect all values, all reasons why God is worshipped. Therefore, there is also no idea of deification. The prophet of the Qur'an is not God, but only the messenger and servant of God ("*rasul*"). One prophet who maintained that he was God was hanged. (ENGINEER)

2. "Anthropic" and "Anthropocentric"

Concerning Horuzhy's terminology, D'SA emphasized that a distinction must be made between "anthropic" and "anthropocentric." The former means only "going out from man," whereas anthropocentrism ascribes to man the central position within the world.

There are several arguments for an anthropocentric position, but only one is compelling: Anthropocentrism cannot be avoided. Phenomenology shows that man is always restricted by the horizon of his experience. This phenomenological anthropocentrism, however, does not establish anthropocentrism in general and, therefore, also not religious anthropocentrism, which is a stronger claim. (HORUZHY)

ENGINEER emphasized that the Qur'an does not advocate anthropocentrism. It is only anthropic, in so far as inspiration can be received only by human beings.

3. Self-Concentration

In response to a comment from the audience that nature has been considered to be holy in the Orthodox tradition, although the religion itself is God-centered, HORUZHY answered that Orthodox Christianity is very much centered on the human self. Its core is a constant prayer. Only if the human person attains an extremely high degree of self-concentration is it possible for him to care for the environment.

NATURALISM AND HUMANISM IN CREATION
AND CONSTRUCTION IN HINDUISM

D. P. Chattopadhyaya

1. Creation and Construction

To start with, the important distinction drawn between *creation* and *construction* needs to be borne in mind. Construction presupposes some prior plan or design of action. In executing that plan, some external materials, means, or agencies are required and deployed. A paradigmatic use of the term *construction* is to be found in the context of architecture and building. Here one needs not only a blueprint but also some materials to give shape to or work out that blueprint. For example, to build a house or mansion, the builder needs the help of an architect, a contractor, and suppliers of different materials. In the work of construction the concerned person cannot work in isolation. He needs others' help and expertise.

In the act of creation the creator is supposed to be more or less free. It is said in many religious theories that God has created the world out of his own will. Out of nothing he brings it into existence. What is implied is that his act of creation is not conditioned by any external will or agency. Of course, it has been pointed out by some thinkers that God's creation is "in accordance" with the nature of the actions (*karma*) which individuals (*jīvas*) have performed in their previous births. According to the law of *karma,* since every individual, for the sake of justice, is required to enjoy or suffer the results of his action (*karma-phala*), God creates the world accordingly. But this "accordance," it is claimed, does not compromise God's freedom, creative freedom.

To take another example, the poet or the painter is said to be free in his creative work. His creative impulse or genius (*pratibhā)* is not traceable to any external compulsion. It is likened to a spiritual upsurge, God's self-initiated will to create the universe. The critic points out the limits of the analogy between *divine* creation and *artistic* creation. While God is all-comprehensive, leaving nothing outside him to interfere with his creativity, it is argued, the same cannot be said of the artist who, unlike God, is finite and fallible. This disanalogy is often extended further by highlighting the distinction between the God's *native* and *perfect* aesthetic (all-beautiful) nature and the artist's *acquired* and *imperfect* aesthetic disposition. Furthermore, it has been pointed out that the artist's

P. Koslowski (eds), Nature and Technology in the World Religions, 83–98.

themes, though more or less mediated and transformed, are traceable to his social milieu, cultural tradition, and natural environment. However, the key concept in the context of creation remains freedom, despite its attending limitation in the case of human beings, because of their socio-historical and natural-environmental situatedness.

2. Technology and Art

The relation between construction or its Sanskrit equivalent, *nirmāṇa*, and creation or its Sanskrit equivalent, *sṛṣṭi*, brings to one's mind the relation between technology and art. One of the many well known definitions of the term "man" is "tool-using animal" or "*homo technicus*." It is interesting to recall that the Sanskrit word *kalā* and the Greek word *techne* (τέχνη) both mean (in English) *art*. Furthermore, it may be noted that the Sanskrit word *takṣan*, the Greek word *tekton* (τέιτον), and the Avestan word *taśan* are associated with such words as "carving," "crafting," and "skillful work." Other cognates of the artist are "carpenter," "craftsman," "artisan," "smith," "master" (Russian "*masterovoj*") and Sanskrit *kāru* (doer, maker) from the verbal root *kṛ* (do, make).

Another point to be noted here is that the distinction between *fine art* and *practical art* was not insisted upon in ancient times. For example, the current distinction between the technique of the goldsmith and that of the poet was either unknown or largely ignored. The underlying assumption seems to be that a kind of skill was at work in both cases. It suggests that the *pratibhā-* (*genius-*) like *free* and *spontaneous* faculty was not always recognized.

In the context of creation, the concepts of *artist* and *craftsman* and their surrogates are extremely important. In the Hindu tradition, the God Viśvakarmā is the presiding deity simultaneously of (i) world creation (*viśva-sṛṣṭi*), (ii) machines and engineering, and (iii) sixty-four kinds of arts, from music, dance, and painting to resolution of poetic problems, expertise in sports, and knowledge of preparing encyclopedias. The point to be noted here is that the distinction between what I have referred to by terms like *construction* (*nirmāṇa*) and *creation* (*sṛṣṭi*) is underplayed in the classical Indian tradition. At the same time, one notices its differential approach to what is created by God (e.g., the universe) and what is constructed by the artist or artisan (e.g., *carpentry*, *architecture*, and *poetry*).

3. Preliminary Comments about Hinduism

Before I say something specifically about the Hindu view of creation (of the world or universe), some preliminaries need to be stated. Hinduism does not represent a unified corpus of thoughts and practices. It is well known that the very word "*Hindu*" is a phonetic variation of the word "*Sindhu*," which stands in Sanskrit-linked languages for both sea or ocean (in a generic sense) and a particular river, the Indus, of North-West India. The West Asians and Ionians used to pronounce *sa* as *ha*. Hence, the peoples who came both before and after the Christian era from Ionia and the West Asian countries used to refer to the peoples living in the Sindhu (Indus) valley as Hindu. The expression "*Hindu*" does not stand for a unified ethnic group. It refers to many ethnic groups, such as the Austrics, Dravidians, Aryans, and Mongoloids. Each one of these is heterogeneous. Both philological and anthropological evidence, based on archaeological data, support this view.

From the religious point of view, Hinduism does not represent a single unified view. It represents a set of views, values, and rituals. Those who are commonly known as Hindu do not have any Bible-like or Koran-like text. Nor do they have any single spiritual head. Nor do they have a *single* Vatican-like or Mecca-like seat of authority or sacred place of pilgrimage. Yet it would not be unfair to affirm that there is a loose kind of unity in the views, values, rituals, and religious beliefs of the peoples professing Hinduism. This unity is most frequently, not necessarily, traced to the Vedic corpus, comprising four Vedas, Upaniṣads and Purāṇas. Scrutiny of the contents of these sacred works, *Śrutis* (what has been heard) and *Smṛtis* (what has been remembered), shows that Hinduism comprises many Vedic, pre-Vedic, and non-Vedic views and practices.

4. Hindu Theories of Creation

Hindu views of creation are numerous. It would be wrong to maintain that one would find a single theory of creation in Hindu thought. At the same time, one may plausibly argue that the pre-Vedic, Vedic, Upaniṣadic, Purāṇic, and even non-Vedic views of creation can be brought together and reconstructed as a familial whole. Due to long and tolerant interaction between them, a kind of family resemblance is found in these views.

The Hindu views of creation are to be found in seminal form in the hymns of the *Ṛgveda*. In the first chapter (*vide* 164th hymn or *sūkta*) it is said that "ultimate reality is one but the learned persons name it differently." Then again in the 58th *sūkta* of Chapter (*Maṇḍala*) 8 we read, "One or It pervades everything." This monistic view has been restated somewhat more explicitly in the Nēsadīya Hymn (*Maṇḍala* 10). It has been translated differently by scholars such as Max Müller[1] and H. H. Wilson.[2] In Müller's translation, the Nāsadīya hymn takes the following form:

> There was then neither what is nor what is not, there was no sky, nor the heaven which is beyond. What covered? Where was it, and in whose shelter? Was the water the deep abyss (in which it lay)?

> There was no death, hence was there nothing immortal. There was no light (distinction) between night and day. That One breathed by itself without breath, other than it there has been nothing.

> Darkness there was, in the beginning all this was a sea without light; the germ that lay covered by the husk, that One was born by the power of heat (*tapas*).

> Love overcome it in the beginning, which was the seed springing from mind, poets having searched in their heart found by wisdom the bond of what is in what is not.

> Their ray which was stretched across, was it below or was it above? There were seed-bearers, there were powers, self-power below, and will above.

> Who then knows, who has declared it here, from whence was born this creation? The gods came later than this creation, who then knows whence it arose?

> He from whom this creation arose, whether he made it or did not make it, the highest seer in the highest heaven, he forsooth knows, or does even he not know?

From this Vedic version of creation one gets a highly metaphysical account of creation. In it the ultimate reality has not been affirmed either as *being* or as *non-being*. The categories of *existence* and *non-existence* are also not affirmed. This suggests the impredicable or unspeakable nature of that Reality from which this universe, marked by ontological multiplicity, has proceeded.

Attempts have been made by some modern scholars to give a scientific interpretation of this metaphysical theory. They try to bring it close to the notion of primeval dense matter, which knows no difference in it and through which no light could initially penetrate. Whether telescoping an up-to-date cosmological view into the Vedic thinkers is correct or incorrect will be clear only in the future. The supporters of this interpretation take the epistemological stand that the ancient sages, endowed with paranormal intuitive power, had their direct cognitive access to Reality (in the form of self-realization). This form of cognition may be described as knowledge-by-identity.

It must be added here that this monistic or absolutistic account of creation is not the only one to be found in the Vedic literature. In some of the hymns two

---

[1] See S. Radhakrishnan, *Indian Philosophy*, Vol. 1 (London: George Allen & Unwin, 1948), pp. 100-102.

[2] H. H. Wilson, *Works*, ed., W. F. Webster, Vol. 6 (Delhi: Nag Publishers, 1990), pp. 434-38.

principles, *Puruṣa* (Self) and *Prakṛti* (Nature) are posited (10th *Maṇḍala, 82, 5-6*). The primitive germ of creation, it is believed, was contained within *Prakṛti*. This particular hymn, dedicated to *Viśvakarman*, states that the first germ, *Brahmāṇḍa* [Brahman-as-seed or -egg] was floating on the waters, representing the principle of the world of life. From this world emerges *Viśvakarman*, the maker or architect of the world. Both in Greek thought (e.g., Thales) and in the book of *Genesis*, comparable accounts of creation are found. In the depth of elements like Water was lodged such creative principles as *Desire, Mind, Will*, or a personal God like *Nārāyaṇa* (identified with *Brahmā* or *Viṣṇu*). In the mythical image of *Viṣṇu* in the bed of Water (*Jaladhi Śayana*) we find a dualistic picture of creation. In Indian thought both of these streams, *Absolutism* and *Dualism, Spiritualism* and *Naturalism,* the former represented by the Vedantic schools and the latter by the Sāṁkhya schools, are discernibly available.

5. Hindu Schools and their Theories of Creation

In Hindu thought, as said above, there are different theories of creation. The leading ones are (1) Sāṁkhya, (2) Yoga, (3) Śaṁkara (Vedānta), (4) Purāṇa, (5) Vaiṣṇava, (6) Śākta, and (7) Grammarian. Each of these schools has been represented differently by different thinkers. These conceptions may be viewed, broadly speaking, under two heads: primarily Vedic and primarily non-Vedic. But analysis reveals that their similarity is due to the effects of mutual interaction over the centuries. Because of obvious constraints of time and space, I propose to present only some of these views, and very briefly.

5.1. THE SCHOOL OF SĀṀKHYA

The name of the system, Sāṁkhya, is said to be derived from the word Saṁkhyā, which means number. Some thinkers have referred to the similarity (understood in terms of mathematizability) between Pythagoreanism and Sāṁkhya thought. The latter has undergone different phases. Its older phase is to be found in the Mahābhārata, the Bhagavatapurāṇa, and the Viṣṇupurāṇa. The main thesis of the Sāṁkhya view is that the immediate causes of the creation of the world, *Puruṣa* (Spirit) and *Prakṛti* (Nature), are potentially contained in God (*Īśvara*) as his two aspects. At the time of *pralaya* or dissolution, *Puruṣa* and *Prakṛti* remain unrelated to each other. When the process of creation begins, God brings them together by his creative power, called *Time (Kāla)*. This creative power disturbs the state of equilibrium of Nature, consisting of three Guṇas or qualities (disclosiveness, inertia, and dynamism or restlessness). It must be said here that Spirit, strictly speaking, is conceived in its plurality, not as a singular principle. The whole of Nature is for the enjoyment (and suffering) of the Spirits according to their past moral deserts. From this position the early Sāṁkhya writers (such as Īśvara Kṛṣṇa) infer that there is a distinct teleological element in this otherwise naturalistic view.

As a result of the disturbed equilibrium of Nature due to its proximity to and affinity with Spirit(s), the process of evolution is set into motion. The first evolute is *Mahat* (Vastness) or *Buddhi* (Intelligence). The intelligent principle is pervasive and present in *all* Spirits. From Intelligence/Vastness evolves individualism (*ahaṁkāra*). From the disclosive or *sāttvika* individualism emerge eleven organs: five of sense, five of action, and Mind (*Manas*), the only internal organ. From the inert individualism or *tāmasika ahaṁkāra* evolve the five subtle elements (*tanmātrās*), viz., sound, touch, colour, taste, and smell. The restless individualism or *rājasika ahaṁkāra* does not give rise to any particular evolute. It only energises the evolutes of the disclosive and the inert individualisms.

From the subtle elements emerge five classes of atoms of the gross physical elements, viz., ether, air, fire, water, and earth. From the different and varying combination of these physical elements evolves this material universe.

At the time of dissolution (*pralaya*) this process of creation (*sṛṣṭi*) is reversed. All evolutes merge back into the original Nature (*Prakṛti*). The Sāṁkhya thinkers, somewhat like the Vedantic thinkers, believe that effect (*kārya*) resides in cause (*kāraṇa*) before its evolution or emergence. Evolution does not mean a total distinction or break between cause and effect. Therefore, the Sāṁkhya thinkers conclude, creation is a continuous process of the manifestation of the original cause, Nature, into different kinds of evolute.

5.2. THE SCHOOL OF ŚAṀKARA VEDĀNTA

The Sāṁkhya view represents Naturalism; the Vedānta view represents Spiritualism in its most uncompromising form. While the Sāṁkhya system is dualistic or protodualistic, the Vedāntic one is absolutistic. It maintains that ultimate Reality, *Brahman,* is free of all three kinds of differences: intrinsic, homogeneous, and heterogeneous. It may be described as existence (*sat*), consciousness (*cit*), and bliss (*ānanda*). What these words seek to describe is itself ultimate Reality, indivisible (*akhaṇḍa*). Like the Sāṁkhya, the Vedāntin believes that the world of multiplicity and individuality is grounded in what is One and undifferentiated.

The empirical world (*saṁsāra*), though it appears to be real, is found on scrutiny to be unreal. Its ontological status is bivalent, real-unreal. From the practical or *vyvahārika* standpoint of experience-bound human beings, the empirical world studied by science is said to be undoubtedly real. But from the standpoint of the Absolute Reality, the world of science and sense does *not* exist at all. However, it has to be admitted that what exactly expressions like "the stand point of ultimate Reality" mean cannot be coherently stated in intelligible language. The standpoint or positionality of view is unknown to the Brahman or Absolute. Yet, for obvious and pressing practical reason, humans, including the Vedāntins, are obliged to offer an account of the world of science and sense (*saṁsāra*).

In brief, the position is this. Since ultimate Reality knows no difference, change, qualitative or quantitative variation in it, the question of creation or dissolution, strictly speaking, does not arise in Vedāntic thought. Yet, for all of us, the explanation of the changing empirical world is a must, both practically and theoretically. For us finite beings, dream has its Reality. Even shadows are, in a sense, real to us. Extending these analogies, the Vedāntin is obliged to offer an account of creation in terms of the divine power called *māyā*. *Māyā* is again a very difficult concept. In a sense, *māyā is*. Otherwise the creation of world can not be a genuine explanandum. *Māyā* itself is not merely an explanatory or heuristic device. It is more than that. It has an ontological status of its own. From the standpoint of the Absolute, it does *not* exist. *Māyā-śakti* does not belong to Absolute. It is attributed to God. Then, it is claimed, God and Absolute, *Īśvar* and *Brahman,* are essentially identical. What is called God is nothing but Absolute bound by *māyā-śakti*, creative power. Can Absolute be bound by its own *māyā* (power)? Can pure or attributeless Brahman have any power? If so, how? These are some of the very difficult questions that all absolutist theories of creation are bound to face.

Māyā, the creative power of *Īśvara*, consists of three *guṇas* (attributes/constituents), viz., *sattva* (disclosiveness or manifestive urge), *rajas* (restlessness or dynamism), and *tamas* (inertia). Here one notices similarity between the Sāṁkhya concept, *Prakṛti*, and the Vedāntic concept of *Māyā*. But, dissimilarity is equally notable.

From the pure consciousness of Absolute, endowed with the creative power of *māyā*, is produced *ākāśa*. From *ākāśa* arises *vāyu* or air; from *vāyu, tejas* or fire; from *tejas, ap* or water; from *ap, pṛthivī* or earth. All these evolutes are subtle and called (as in Sāṁkhya) *tanmātras*. Initially these five elements remain distinct. Later on, they are mixed up in a fixed proportion called *pañcīkaraṇa*. *Ākāśa* is endowed with *śabda* (sound); *vāyu* (air), with smell and touch; fire with sound, touch and colour (*rūpa*); water with sound, touch, colour and *rasa* (taste); and earth, with sound, touch, colour, taste and *gandha* (smell). Produced by *māyā*, each of these subtle elements is endowed with the three qualities of disclosiveness, restlessness, and inertia.

From disclosive or the expressive aspects of the five subtle elements, taken individually, evolve the five organs of knowledge, viz., hearing, touch, sight, taste, and smell. From the same subtle elements, taken jointly, evolve the internal organs of intelligence, mind, ego-sense, and disengaged mind (*citta*). From the restless or dynamic subtle elements, taken individually, five organs, viz., mouth, hands, feet, sex-organ, and anus are produced. From the same subtle elements, taken jointly, evolve five vital airs: *prāṇa, apāna, udāna, vyāna,* and *samāna*. These products of the subtle elements form the materials of fine bodies called *sūkṣma-deha* or *liṅga-śarīra*. Thus, the Vedāntin thinks, the unmixed fine elements are the sources of the subtle bodies, having seventeen elements, viz., five sense-organs, five motor-organs, five vital airs, mind, and intelligence. From the five subtle static elements, through the process of *Pañcīkaraṇa* or quintuplication, emerge five gross elements (ether, air, fire, water, and earth). Quintuplication is a particular way of admixture of the above five elements, in which every element contains half of itself, while the other half consists of four equal portions of the other four elements.

Contrary to the popular view, the Vedāntin, who believes in the primacy of consciousness as ultimate Reality, takes keen interest in the world of sense and science, and in the process of its emergence out of consciousness. In fact, some modern philosophers, such as B. N. Seal, have described *māyā* as the principles of materialization. Matter emerges from consciousness through the intervention of *māyā*.

6. Matter, Life, and Mind: Continuous, Independent, or Interdependent?

In whichever way one – theologian, philosopher, or natural scientist – looks at the different levels of Reality, one is obliged to offer an *explanation* of their mutual relations. Mere *description* is insufficient. Explanation is called for. Philosophers, theologians, and even natural scientists have offered diverse explanations of the basis of the proclaimed primacy of one of the above three levels of Reality, matter, life, and mind, and have tried to show that the other two levels are derivative in character. Materialists, Vitalists, and Idealists are equally called upon to account for how their own preferred mode of being is related to the other modes. It must be added here that modes of being need not always be construed as three in number. The number may be more or less. The three modes mentioned above are only illustrative or ideal-typical. Within each mode of being, consciousness, life, or matter, there are different grades. The gradualists, such as the Sāṁkhya and Leibnizians, recognize straightaway that there is no sharp line of demarcation between different grades of beings or evaluations of reality. The law of continuity, not hierarchy, operates in Reality.

There are some scientific philosophers who maintain that there are different worlds, viz., (1) the World of Physics and Chemistry, (2) the World of Psychology and Epistemology, and (3) the World of abstract entities like Concept, Theory, Number, and Musical notation. These Worlds are said to be interrelated by circular causation, upward and downward; from (1) to (3) via (2) and again (3) to (1) via (2). Karl Popper, for example, has developed an elaborate theory along these lines. These worlds are both hierarchical and (due to causal interaction) continuous. In this interaction humans, by their mind and action, play a very important role.

The point which I wish to highlight in this context is this: The accounts of creation can be, and in fact have been, construed in different ways, viz., (i) construction by some Supremely Intelligent Principle, like God, (ii) creation due to Matter or non-teleological Nature through the intervention of some force or *māyā*-like principle, and (iii) creation by human beings. It is clear that these principles are not quite exclusive. For example, there are views according to which Nature is divinely or teleologically guided, or Prakṛti is said to be the Executrix-Force of God himself. Sri Aurobindo has defended this view in his *Life Divine* and other works, such as *The Human Cycle*. All human creations, it has been said, are analogical in character. In other words, whatever humans create are analogies of God's own creation of things and beings of the world.

It is instructive to note that the question of technology is not invoked in the context of God's creation. But technology is central to the context of human creation. The implication is this: God is so powerful, perfect, and all-knowing that whatever he *wills* to create he *can* create, without being aided by any technology. In contrast, humans, being finite and fallible, require external aids for creating most things or objects.

The main question that arises here centres round the issue of determining what is *internal* and what is *external*. God, by definition, is all-comprehensive and there can be nothing external to him. He is all-inclusive. But in the case of man it can be pointed out that many techniques, instruments, and forms of technology that he uses are his own creation or part of his human inheritance. Man may not be God-like *Viśvakarmā* (World-Maker) but he makes his own world, not necessarily imitating God's creation. Particularly in the context of aesthetics, ethics, and religion, i.e., in the context of values, man is credited with the power or genius to create values which are not mere imitations of natural objects or mere transvaluation of the existing or remembered values.

If the supremacy or sovereignty of divine creation has to be defended, it is argued, human creations are to be understood either (a) as unconscious imitations or expressions of what God has already created, or (b) as having been transplanted as innate dispositions in human beings. Alternatively, (c) it has to be conceded that if human creations are really autonomous, not due to God in any way, these are bound to degenerate in the course of time, to remain imperfect and sometimes at variance with God's own design of creation. Alternative (c) appears on reflection to be a stricture against the human use (and possible misuse) of technology. Man's tinkering with what God has done or wants to be done by us, following his guidance, needs to be discouraged. Since, *ex hypoth-*

esi we cannot improve upon God's ways of doing things and shaping beings, it has been argued, we have no business to fiddle with the same.

In the modern world of technological wonders, will we be morally prepared to accept this argument? If not, what is the best possible way of reconciling technology with a religious view of creation?

7. Technology and the Creation of Values

Technology may be approached, broadly speaking, from two different points of view: religious and scientific. Different religions – Hinduism, Christianity and Buddhism, for example – do not advocate one unified view on the subject. This is true in almost all major religions. What is very problematic, as I have indicated before with special reference to Hinduism, is that there are diverse, almost contrary, approaches even within it. One can seek to remove these difficulties only by interpretations or glosses.

A similar problem is encountered in science. But the scope of interpretation is limited in this field. Scientific theories of creation, as we know, are quite different. The more famous ones are (i) "unique creation," based on the Second Law of Thermodynamics and (ii) "continuous creation." The defenders of unique creation claim that the process (the increase of entropy with which the law is concerned) could not have an unlimited past and cannot have an unlimited future. The implication is clear: creation begins and ends in time. If the cited law of thermodynamics entails drift towards uniformity and homogeneity, we have to recognize an eventual thermal death of the created universe. The recession of the galaxies, leading to the expansion of the universe, seems to suggest the existence of a primordial state of immense density. One may recall in this connection the Vedic reference to the impenetrable primordial darkness. And that state was the centre of gradual expansion and subsequent dispersion.

The defenders of the theory of "continuous creation" maintain that the recession of the galaxies does not disturb the cosmic status-quo, for new matter in the form of hydrogen atoms is created in sufficient quantity. Neither of these two theories, "unique" and "continuous," is testable. But they do have their importance in the context of cosmological, as distinguished from theological or mythological creation. Unless creation accounts for the harmonious existence of matter, life, and mind, the related theories hardly exhibit any religious implication. Neither recession of the galaxies nor their steady state can be attributed to any intelligent or providential principle. All of these phenomena are explained in terms of value-neutral and mechanically-operative thermal laws. The hard-headed scientist tends to stick to his position that cosmological theories of creation have no theistic implications. But they do not have any reason, certainly not a good reason, to dispute the relevance of creation, creativity, and kindred concepts to the ideas of human freedom, spiritual vision, moral criticism, imagination, and ideas of inventiveness.

Technology, like science, may also be interpreted in two different ways: value-neutrally and in a value-loaded manner. In its simplest form, technology is *neutral* to the purposes of man and his ways of living. Even the use of hands, fingers, feet, and other organs may be viewed as the technological extension of human existence. History and biographical literature inform us of very many extraordinarily gifted persons who were deaf, dumb, blind, or even totally paralyzed. One can easily imagine valued human existence without this or that organ and its uses. At the same time, it remains true that every organ, sense, or motor, external or internal, extends the reach of human being. The *doings* of a human being are not essential to the latter. One remains a human being without doing this or that thing, without using this or that organ. To take an extreme case in order to make the point plain: a *yogi* can calm down his mind to such an ideal state of peacefulness that it may be free of all impressions and tendencies, *vṛttis* and *saṁskāras*, and yet he can at will exercise his cognitive, motor, and other human capacities well. The Buddhist speaks of void consciousness, consciousness devoid of object and content (*viṣaya-śūnya citta*). It is also a typical *yogic* concept. Mind (consciousness) or *citta* may remain what it is, with its potentiality to do many things intact, but actually do nothing.

This point brings me to Heidegger's well-known concept of "standing reserve." A piece of equipment, for example, does not cease to be a piece of equipment, even if it is not put to its *possible* uses. A piece of equipment is a "standing reserve."

Extending this suggestion, one can affirm that human consciousness itself or a human person him/herself is a "standing reserve." Many of its *possibilities*, almost infinite in number, are held back into it without actualizing the same. From this point of view, the human mind can be viewed as a piece of technological equipment, without compromising its dignity. It is true that, ordinarily, this is not how human consciousness is conceived. But that is an incidental, not essential, issue.

Let me revert to the concept of God as creator. God is not externally compelled or obliged to create the world, although he can and does create it. Before it is actually created, the world is said to be mind-born (*mānas-putra*) in God as consciousness.

8. Creator, Creation and the Diversity and Unity of Creatures

Like the Hindu's, the Christian's world is the creation of God. But according to the *Vedāntic* tradition, beyond God is Brahman, without which God is inconceivable. While Brahman is beyond space, time, and causality, God as "the materializing principle" or Pure Consciousness or Brahman, works within the self-imposed framework of space, time, and causality. God may be viewed as *Viśvakarmā*, author of the World. It may remind one of Plato's concept of Demiurge, developed in the *Timaeus*, who, as a subordinate deity, brings eternal *forms* and resistant *matter* together. Brahman is immaterial. As Pure Consciousness, Brahman is not only immaterial but also without form.

In the ancient religious systems of thought, Hinduism, Judaism, and Christianity, one finds two different tendencies: (i) dualism, which affirms two basic principles, and/or (ii) emanationism, which views the world as an efflux of the One. Some forms of Indian religion, Neo-Platonism (particularly Plotinus), Spinoza, and Hegel maintain that particular things of the world emerge out of the One as light comes out of the sun. Individual beings, divorced from their original source, i.e., One, are alien and imperfect, if not negative.

The Hebrew view, in contrast, maintains that the world is a necessary emanation and that creation is a free and personal activity disclosive of the wisdom and power of the creator. God's creative activity in relation to the world, comprising its creatures, is *continuous* in character. It is the sacred responsibility of man to maintain this process of creation. The relation between God and Man is asymmetrical. While the former is independent of the latter, the latter is dependent upon the former.

In the Hindu tradition we come across two strands of thought. In the pure *Vedāntic* strand of thought, the thesis of asymmetry, God's independence, is affirmed. But in the *Vaiṣṇava* strand of thought, in which the concept of God's *līlā* (or playfulness) plays an important role, the symmetry thesis, the interdependence of God and Man, is highlighted.

In the Christian tradition one also finds two strands of thought: dualistic and monistic. According to the Logos idea of the Apostle John, the *eternal* Creator-God incarnates himself in history, making a new creation among mankind. But the Gnostic view, the first phase of Christianity, largely influenced by the Hellenized Near East, was radically dualistic. It is the dualism between Man and the World, and between the World and God. In either case, it is a dualism of an antithetical, not complementary, kind. Irenaeus's (a 2nd-century Church Father's) doctrine of "creation *ex nihilo*" seeks to oppose Gnostic dualism, affirming that God created out of nothing and thus transcends both his creation and creatures.

In the subsequent development of Christianity, the influence of Hellenic Philosophy is unmistakable. Plato's philosophical theory of ideal forms is assimilated into the Christian doctrine of creation. St. Augustine provides the lead in this direction. Plato's ideal forms become archetypal ideas in the mind of God, which, at creation, were implicitly implanted in Nature, thereby making the natural world the orderly, law-governed, and intelligible revelation of his wisdom and goodness.

Later on, St. Thomas Aquinas assimilates some Platonic insights and many Aristotelian ideas into Christian philosophy. He seeks to resolve the conflict between reason and revelation. He conceives the Creator as the incarnate Logos. He thinks that the essence of God is to *exist* and to lend existence to other things. But this doctrine cannot be convincingly established by philosophy or rational enquiry. The truth of these views, in their fullness, is available only in revelation. Rational philosophy enables man only to understand revealed doctrine, but it cannot demonstrate it.

The emergence of the mechanical concept of Nature, largely due to Descartes and Newton, obviously posed a big problem to the Christian modes of philosophy and religion. The response was two-fold: mathematical and experiential, and, at times, a combination of the two. The rational-mathematical attempt (better known as Rationalism) was to show that the orderliness of nature is expressive of God's own perfect nature. The empiricist, without rejecting the idea of the rationality of nature, highlighted the law-connectable character of whatever is experienceable: primary (geometrical) qualities and secondary (sense) qualities of objects. Since the Cartesian-Newtonian days, the 17th-18th centuries, no explicit Christian attempt is evident to reject totally the mechanical view of nature.

To mitigate the fallout of mechanism in religion, religious thinkers, aware of modern scientific development, have highlighted the concepts of law-governed orderliness and the presence (direct or indirect) of God in nature. The concepts of grace, revelation, and intuition have also received overriding attention in this context. The whole exercise is intended to bring modern science close to religion and to infuse the former with religious values, representing natural human cravings for an enlightened and harmonious life. It aims to show the harmony between naturalism and humanism, and to counter the commonsense belief that *mechanical* nature is stepmotherly, i.e., hostile, to human efforts to be free and successful value-seekers.

9. A Hindu (rather Indian) Religio-Philosophical View Seeking to Integrate Naturalism, Humanism, and Technology

By religion I understand *dharma*, which involves a set of beliefs and supernatural power or powers, the will to stand well with that power or powers, and practices devoted to this end. The most common semantic source of "religion" or *dharma* is "belief," "faith," but a few are based on "worship," service of "god," or "insight." The other common etymological root of *dharma*, *dhṛ* (from Sanskrit) and *religio* (from Latin) suggests some "binding power" or "path to God or Gods." It is interesting to note that most Indo-European roots of the word God (*devatā*) or its synonyms are traceable to "light" or "day" (e.g., Grk.

dios, Skt. *dyaus*, Latin *deiuos*, Irish *dia*, Lith. *dievas*). So *dharma* is seeking of light or enlightenment (*Buddhatva*). If one accepts this notion/definition of religion or *dharma*, it may be interpreted in either of two ways: with God or without God (as in Buddhism). Generally speaking, it is safe to take religions as the quest for fundamental values, such as freedom – freedom toward light from the darkness of ignorance, harmony as freedom from disorderliness, peace as freedom from pain and restlessness, and development as freedom from degeneration or growthlessness.

If these values are recognized as basic values of human beings in civil society, one finds that technology, in its positive sense, is not inimical to the pursuit of these values. On the contrary, technology contributes much to the promotion of the said values. For example, from the most painful dis-value, called disease or illness, we need the help of medicine, surgery, psychiatry, physio-therapy, artificial limbs, and many other mechanical devices for diagnostic or detective purposes. To be free from disease seems to be the basic freedom, freedom-as-value for every embodied creature.

Secondly, we seek knowledge or light in order to be free from the darkness of ignorance. In Hinduism and many other religions, one of the basic prayers is: "Take us from darkness to light" (*tamaso mā jyotirgamaya*). In realizing this goal of light or knowledge, technology has been of immense help. In the modern era of printing and information technology, many of us forget that even writing, the invention of the alphabet, and the use of the writing or inscriptional devices of hoary antiquity were great technological inventions. In our drive for literacy, computer literacy, and distant education, we do need, and are making use of, various sorts of technology. The "standing reserve" of technology is far-reaching and limitless in its consequences.

Thirdly, to fight another dis-value, poverty, we have used technology quite extensively. Poverty has been and continues to be a curse to a large section of mankind. If we really believe in the unity of mankind, we must admit that so long as a large section of it remains in ignorance and suffers from poverty, our proclaimed religious ends, universal enlightenment, universal development, and other similar values are bound to remain unrealized. In the last fifty years or so, we may easily recall how much development has taken place in the fields of agriculture and industry. For this development, the contribution of technology has been very significant. In irrigation, plant biology, and various other related fields of agriculture, mankind has been immensely benefited by technology.

Fourthly and finally, the most important values are not merely what may be called *freedom-from*. *Freedom-toward* is equally, if not more, important. Freedom *from* illness, freedom *from* ignorance, and freedom *from* poverty, for example, are inputs for realizing higher values such as creative leisure, disposition, and action. In a manner of speaking, one might say that technology, rightly used, can free a large section of mankind from many dis-values, disabilities, and diseases. Normatively speaking, technology can take man to the highest heights of development.

When I refer to this positive and normative aspects of technology, I do not, or rather we should not, remain indifferent to its negative fallouts. For example, excessive dependence on technology takes away, or at least adversely affects, our natural abilities. Many of our modern diseases are due to a lack of normal exercise or work habits.

Secondly, technology is bound to have its *alienating* impact on our nature. When the machine is allowed to mediate excessively in the area of inter-individual human relationships, the latter tend to become increasingly impersonal, almost mechanical.

Thirdly, technology encourages passivity and lack of creativity. Given to passive entertainment provided by telecommunication, many of us have unconsciously lost our interest in active and creative works.

Fourthly, since technology can deliver "miracles," modern civilizations, particularly the affluent sections, are silently engaged in a *conflict* to develop, possess, control, and use the latest forms of technology. As I said above, since the "standing reserve" of technology is immense, it is natural for greedy and rich people to run after the most developed technology. In the process, disputes over copyrights, patent rights, and other similar sensitive issues are bound to increase, both intranationally and transnationally. The future of the World Trade Organization (WTO) will also be increasingly dispute-oriented. Unless the *harmony* between rich and poor, the developed and the developing nations, can be rationally and justly sorted out, the effect of technology may not be as beneficial as we expect it to be.

Fifthly, one of the most negative aspects of technology is its possible misuse for the purpose of *domination over nature*. It is by mastering the laws and forces of nature through science and philosophy that we are extracting so much from nature. In the Hindu tradition, the world is said to be *Vasundharā, Vasudhā,* and *Vasumatī.* All of these synonyms are based on the recognition of the world as *vasu* or resource, treasure and wealth. If the misuse of technology results in increasingly depleting natural resources, we, or rather our descendants, will be poorer in the future. In the ways we are using our technology and exploiting the resources of nature today, responsible environmentalists tell us, we are plundering the world and endangering the future of mankind. One must add here that this is not an inevitable process. If we all really believe that this planet is our common village, our only habitat, we must use our technology in a truly responsible and constructive manner.

Sixthly and finally, the other and perhaps the most dangerous aspect of modern technology is found in the field of nuclear armaments. The most tragic events of the 20th century have been two world wars and the dropping of two atomic bombs on civilian targets. Even after that, trillions of dollars have been spent annually on nuclear armaments, developing deadly weapon systems and fearful deterrents; we are not sure of our security, national or global. At the same time, millions of people had been suffering from poverty, famine, and malnutrition. Attempts are made to justify dangerously high expenditures in the arms industry in the name of security. In fact, technology is being used for economic hegemony over the globe.

But, as I said before, the misuse of technology is no argument against its good use.

VENERATION OF NATURE, USE OF NATURE, AND SELF-IMPROVEMENT OF HUMANKIND BY TECHNOLOGY IN THE ŚRAMAṆA TRADITION (BUDDHISM AND JAINISM)

Shivram S. Antarkar

1. The Śramaṇic Weltanschauung [1]

1.1. ŚRAMAṆA AS RELIGIOUS WELTANSCHAUUNG AND WAY OF LIFE

Buddhism and Jainism, the two non-theistic living faiths, originated in India more than 2,500 years ago. While Hinduism belongs to the Vedic tradition, these two faiths belong to the non-Vedic tradition, known as the Śramaṇa tradition.

The Śramaṇa tradition did not accept the authority of the *Vedas*, nor did it accept the belief in the personal God or impersonal Brahman. However, Śramaṇic atheism or non-theism is not a form of irreligion. The word from the Indian languages that comes closest in meaning to the word "religion" is "*dharma*" (Sanskrit) or "*dhamma*" (Prakrit). The Śramaṇa tradition is a religious tradition in so far as it grapples with the problems of suffering, sin, and evil in the world and the means of ultimate or final redemption or deliverance from them, as all religions do. This deliverance is called *nirvāṇa* or *mokṣa*. The Śramaṇa tradition, however, grapples with the same religious problems in a conceptual framework or with a paradigm totally different from the one accepted by the theistic religions and, hence, could dispense with God. In so far as it shares with other religions "*weltschmerz*,"[2] i.e. a vague yearning and discontent with regard to the general condition of human existence and the constitution of the world, and propounds a comprehensive world-outlook or world-vision to liberate humanity from this deplorable condition, it is a religious *weltanschauung* – a religious way of life.

---

[1] Cf. G. C. Pande, *Śramaṇa Tradition: Its History and Contribution to Indian Culture* (Ahmadabad: L. D. Institute of Indology, 1978), p. 1.

[2] Ibid., p. 9.

99

P. Koslowski (eds), Nature and Technology in the World Religions, 99–120.
© 2001 *Kluwer Academic Publishers. Printed in the Netherlands.*

1.2. REJECTION OF GOD AS CREATOR AND CUSTODIAN OF THE MORAL LAW – THE CENTRALITY OF KARMA

Generally, God is accepted in order to provide satisfactory answers to the four perennial philosophical problems which have disturbed thinkers all over the world.

(a) The first problem may be called "the riddle of the universe" – the question about the why and how of the universe. When and how has the universe come into existence? What was there before the universe came into existence? What is its cause? Who created it? Why is it there at all? The theistic religions have answered these questions in terms of the omniscient, omnipotent, and kind person called God. This answer, regarded as a rational explanation of the existence of the universe, justified and justifiable by logical arguments, is, however, found wanting and unsatisfactory. It raises more questions than it answers. Many philosophers, including Kant and Hegel, have argued that rational arguments to prove the existence of God are, to say the least, inconclusive. Human reason seems to be incapable of giving a satisfactory answer. It cannot be the infallible guide to give answers to the ultimate questions about Cosmos, God, and Soul.

(b) This leads the theist to accept God as the infallible source of knowledge who reveals the truth to human beings through prophets. Thus God is accepted both as the creator and as the infallible source of knowledge. The Asian mind in general and the Indian mind in particular is not committed to theism. The Hindu attitude is ambivalent on the problem of God. But the Śramaṇa attitude is definitely against accepting any creator God. The atheistic or non-theistic religions and philosophies dispense with God by rejecting the assumption that the universe has a beginning or that it is created or caused. The universe, the Indian religions hold, is either eternal (*nitya*) or beginningless (*anādi*). It is either eternally there or, time being infinite, it makes no sense to talk of the first moment of time. Moreover, the notion of empty time when nothing existed is also not intelligible. In short, the Śramaṇa tradition does not accept the idea of a creator God. It also believes that human beings have the potentiality of achieving omniscience. The present limitations on the human faculty of knowing are due to the fact that the pure cognitive faculty of the spirit is covered and distorted by an alien matter. When a person purifies the spirit or consciousness, he achieves enlightenment or absolute knowledge or omniscience. Such a liberated person is the infallible source of knowledge. Hence, the Śramaṇa tradition can dispense with God as an infallible source of knowledge also.

(c) The third consideration which forces the theist to accept God is that many good and virtuous persons who deserve happiness are found to suffer, while those who are wicked and vicious are found to prosper in our society. Our moral reason, however, demands that a wicked person deserves to be punished and the virtuous to be rewarded. The theist, therefore, argues that though the natural law, and the socio-political legal system are unable to give fruits of good and bad actions to the agents according to what they morally deserve, God preserves the moral law by rewarding and punishing the persons according to their deserts, if not during this life, in their existence after death. Thus God is the moral governor who safeguards the moral law by justly rewarding and punishing persons for their actions by taking into consideration their motives, intentions, circumstances, etc.

The Śramaṇa tradition dispenses with God as the moral governor by accepting the law of karma. The law of karma is accepted by the Hindu theists also. It is a common belief shared by all of the religions that originated in India. According to the law of karma, every action, good or bad, produces its pleasurable or painful effects at an appropriate time. Both the Śramaṇa and the Vedic traditions accept the theory of rebirth. Each individual receives appropriate fruit – reward or punishment – of his good or bad actions. It is the effects of these actions that determine future life. The pleasures and sufferings in the present are due to the actions in the previous life.

(d) Lastly, the theist believes that it is by surrendering to God and obeying his commandments that an individual can attain salvation. God's grace plays an important and indispensable role in the path of salvation. The Śramaṇa tradition, on the contrary, holds that the individual by his own ignorance and consequent craving and attachment gets bound, and he can by right faith, right knowledge, and right conduct achieve liberation.

1.3. ŚRAMA, ŚAMA, SAMA: SELF-EFFORT, SELF-CONTROL, EQUANIMITY

It is this emphasis on self-effort (*śrama*) that explains the significance of the term "*Śramaṇa*." The Sanskrit term "*Śramaṇa*" becomes "*Samana*" in Prakrit. Scholars have understood the term "*Samana*" in three ways. It is the tradition which lays emphasis on (i) self-effort, (*śrama*), (ii) self-control (*śama*), and (iii) equality and equanimity (*sama*). These three aspects are the *sine qua non* of the Śramaṇic weltanschauung. It is atheistic or non-theistic. It is also mainly a monastic tradition. The doctrines of karma, the cycle of birth and death, and deliverance from this cycle constitute the essence of the Śramaṇic belief system.

1.4. SPIRITUAL INDIVIDUALISM

The Śramaṇa tradition is as old as the Vedic tradition. It emphasises self-effort, self-control, and equanimity. It does not have any room for God and grace. It recommends asceticism. In the Vedic tradition, religion and morality are essentially tied with the maintenance of social life. In contrast "Śramaṇism is an extreme form of spiritual individualism which has even been called soteriological egoism."[3] Śramaṇism was never one school or one organised religion. There were many small sects of mendicants organised around some influential teachers. There was even antagonism between the different Śramaṇic sects. In the sixth century B.C., some important sects were Ājīvika, Niggantha, Śākya, Tāpasa, and Gairika. From among these sects, the Niggantha and the Śākya were organised and further developed mainly by the two great personalities of the sixth century B.C., Vardhamāna Mahāvira and Siddhārtha Gautama, into what are now known as Jainism and Buddhism.

These two historical figures were contemporaries. They belonged to the sixth century B. C. Both hailed from the north-eastern part of India – the present state of Bihar. Both belonged to royal warrior families. Both had happy childhood and happy married lives. However, neither of them could find satisfaction in the worldly life, power, and riches. Their real interest was the quest for spiritual salvation. They, therefore, relinquished family life, power, and riches, became ascetics, practised penance, meditation, etc., conquered themselves, achieved spiritual wisdom, preached for several years, and passed away leaving behind the great religio-spiritual legacy which their followers even today follow with admiration, devotion, and faith. Though the general tenor of their weltanschauung is more or less similar, their specific tenets and practices are different and even partly antagonistic. It would, therefore, be fruitful to know about their lives, teachings, and the fundamental tenets and practices of their respective religions.

2. Jainism

2.1. MAHĀVIRA'S LIFE

Vardhamāna Mahāvira (599-527 B.C.)[4] was the son of Siddhārtha and Triśsālā. Since his father was a chief of the clan of Jnatrikas, he was brought up in a royal family as a prince. He was married and had a daughter. But he did not find satisfaction in the worldly life. At the age of thirty, after the death of his parents, he embraced the life of a monk. He followed the practices of the Niggantha sect, which had been organised by an ascetic named Pārśva about two centuries earlier. "Niggantha" means "free from the knot of bondage." Pārśva prescribed fourfold controls (Cāturyāma dharma) – namely non-violence, non-

---

[3] Ibid., p. 41.

[4] There are conflicting accounts of Mahāvira's life and controversies about the dates. This account is based mainly on Sinclair Stevenson, *The Heart of Jainism* (New Delhi: Munshiram Manoharlal, 1995) and partly on A. L. Basham, *The Wonder that Was India* (Bombay: Rupa and Co., 1967).

lying, non-stealing, and non-possession.

Vardhamāna wandered from place to place for twelve years, begging his food, doing penance and meditation, and subjecting his body and mind to varieties of austerities. At first he wore a single white piece of cloth. But after thirteen months, he renounced that also and lived for the rest of his life in complete nudity.

In the thirteenth year of his asceticism, Vardhamāna conquered himself completely and became a "conqueror" (*Jina*), worthy of veneration (*arhat*), a destroyer of enemies in the form of passions, temptations, etc., (*arihanta*), and a "ford-maker" (*Tirthankara*). He soon became popular and had a large following. He taught his religion for thirty years and at the age of seventy-two left his body and achieved final liberation (*mokṣa*). The follower of Jina is called Jaina. The religion (*dhamma*) preached by Jina is called Jaina religion.

Mahāvira is not the founder of the Jaina religion. As stated earlier, he started his spiritual journey by entering into the order of Pārśva. But even Pārśva ātha is not the founder of Jaina religion. The Jaina tradition holds that there were twenty-three Tirthankaras before Mahāvira, and that Pārśvanātha was the twenty-third; the first being Ṛṣabhadeva. A Thirthankara, (generally rendered into English as "Ford-maker") has a special place in the Jaina tradition. He is not only an omniscient (*kevali*) and liberated (*mukta* or *siddha*) soul, but a person who establishes "*tīrtha*," i.e. who shows or makes a passage for crossing the flowing river of transmigration; who preaches, revives, and re-establishes the eternal principles of Jainism according to the place, time, and conditions; and who establishes the four-fold community of monks, nuns, laymen, and laywomen. According to the tradition, Mahāvira is the twenty-fourth Tirthankara. He is believed to be the last Tirthankara in the present cycle of time.

2.2. JAINA PHILOSOPHY AND RELIGION

Jainism divides the whole universe into two main categories – living (*jīva*) and non-living (*ajīva*). Everything that is living is characterised by consciousness (*upayoga*) and the non-living by absence of consciousness. Living beings are infinite in number and are uncreated, eternal, though they undergo birth, death, and change. They are classified into various categories on the basis of (1) mobility, (2) number of sense organs, (3) type of birth, etc.

Jainism treats natural resources like earth, water, fire, air, as well as all types of plants and vegetation as living but immobile. They have very rudimentary consciousness of touch-sensation only. All microbes, insects, worms, birds, animals, human and even infernal and heavenly beings are mobile and possess more than one sense. They are further classified on the basis of number of senses, from two to five, and those who have five senses and mind. Those who have five senses and mind are of three types – infernal, human, and heavenly.

The non-living reals are of five types: matter, medium of motion, medium of rest, space, and time.

Let us first understand the second category of "non-living" (*ajīva*) beings in brief in so far as it is relevant to understand the Jaina view about the nature of humankind and its relation to animal kingdom, plant life, and natural resources such as earth, water, fire, and air. All that exists, exists in space and time. These two categories, therefore, are necessary conditions for all existence. The special feature of the Jaina view of space is that it divides space into occupied space (*lokākāśa*) and absolutely empty or unoccupied space (*alokākāśa*). The former accommodates the infinite number of material objects and atoms, living beings, the media of motion and rest. The occupied space is surrounded by the unoccupied space (*alokākāśa*) which contains nothing – neither matter nor living beings nor even the media of motion and rest. Time is in itself eternal, but chronological time is measured by conventional units and is an auxiliary cause of modifications and changes in all things. Chronological time is cyclic. It is like a wheel that rotates ceaselessly upwards and downwards. It is divided into two half-cycles – descending and ascending. Each half-cycle is further divided into six parts (*ārā*). The present time is the fifth part of the descending half-cycle. Mahāvira is the last Trthankara of this half-cycle.[5] The two categories of the media of motion and rest are peculiar to Jainism. They are not the causes of motion but are only auxiliary conditions which make motion and rest possible.

The most important sub-category of the non-living reals is matter (*pudgala*). Matter has two forms: atomic (*paramāṇu*) and aggregate (*skandha*). In its atomic form it is uncreated and eternal. All atoms are alike, possessing colour, smell, taste, and touch. The aggregates are formed by combination and separation of material particles.

From the eight types of combination of ultimate material particles, eight types of material aggregates are formed, from the gross to the most subtle. They include five types of "body" for living beings, as well as the breathing organs, the speech organs, and mind. The most subtle of them is "karmic body," which a living being carries with it from one life to another.

The term "*jīva*" (living or sentient being) is used in Jainism to refer to both the liberated (*mukta* or *siddha*) souls and the empirical selves living in bondage. According to it, the liberated soul (*mukta jīva*) or soul (*jīva*) in its purity possesses infinite cognition of two types – infinite perception (*darśana*) and infinite knowledge (*jñāna*) infinite energy or power (*vīrya*) and perfect character (*caritra*). Moreover, it has neither birth not death, i.e. it has no finite life-span; no material body. It has infinite bliss but not pleasures and pains, it also has no social or other status. But the empirical self lacks infinite perception and infinite

---

[5] Shah Natubhai, *Jainism: The World of Conquerors*, 2 vols. (Brighton: Sussex Academy Press, 1998), Vol. II, p. 36, Fig. 3.4. See Appendix.

knowledge, infinite energy or power and perfect character. So also it undergoes birth and death, i.e. it has a finite life-span, it possesses a physical body, it enjoys pleasures and suffers pain and has low or high status. These limitations, finitudes, and defilements of the infinite, pure nature of the *jīva* are due to the bondage of karma. The Jain religion, therefore, raises a fourfold enquiry into: the nature of bondage (*bandha*), the cause of bondage (*bandha-hetu*), the nature of liberation (*mokṣa*), and the means of liberation (*mokṣopāya*).

The whole Jaina thought centres round the twin concepts of spiritual bondage and liberation. A living being (*jīva*), by its activity of body, speech, and mind, produces vibrations in the space – points of soul (*ātma-pradeśa*), i.e. in consciousness which occupies the whole body of the individual. Due to these vibrations, subtle material particles, which are fit to become "karma," are attracted by the soul. They enter the space occupied by consciousness. This is called inflow or influx of kārmic matter. Due to perverted vision, passions, attachment, and negligence, these particles become stuck to consciousness and limit, obscure, and defile it. Thus the soul becomes bound; it has to undergo the series of births and deaths in order to reap the fruits of its actions – pleasurable consequences of good and meritorious actions and painful consequences of bad and sinful actions. Thus nobody other than oneself is responsible for one's own plight. One binds oneself due to ignorance, temptations, indulgences, etc.

If a person himself is responsible for bondage, he has to make efforts to attain release from this bondage. Jainism mentions two ways of release: stopping any further influx of kārmic matter (*samvara*), and shedding of past karma (*nirjarā*). Though it is necessary to stop further inflow, it is not sufficient. It must be supported by *nirjarā*, i.e. by shedding of the kārmic matter which has already entered the soul. This is done by penance of various types, austerities, and so on. These practices burn the past karma and purify the soul. When the soul is completely purified by total destruction of all karmas, it becomes omniscient (*kevali*). At this stage four types of karma – the perception and knowledge obscuring karma, the deluding karma which obscures faith and character, and the obstructing karma which affects infinite energy – are destroyed.

But the person continues to live until his other four karmas – determining his (i) life-span, (ii) body, (iii) pleasures and pains, and (iv) family status – are destroyed. A Tirthankara continues to perform his functions as a Tirthankara according to his life-span determining karma. With the total destruction of these four karmas, the person is finally liberated from the cycle of births and deaths; he goes to the place for the liberated soul, which is at the top on the border of occupied and unoccupied space. This is called Siddhaśīla.

The Jaina religion provides an elaborate account of the means by which further influx is to be stopped and the past karma is to be burnt. They include observance of a number of vows, cultivating supreme virtues, observing forbearances and discomforts, practising different types of internal and external austerities, meditation and concentration, and so on.

This brief outline of Jainism may bring home the point that, though atheistic, it is not just a secular ethics but a religion aiming at the supra-ethical, supra-rational goal of spiritual salvation (*mokṣa*). Let us now turn to Buddhism.

3. Buddhism

3.1. THE LIFE OF THE BUDDHA

The only religion that originated in ancient India and then spread outside India and is recognised even today as one of the major world religions, along with Christianity and Islam, is the Buddhist religion. It has assumed this name after the great personality of the sixth century B.C., Siddhārtha Gautama, who after enlightenment was called "the Buddha" – "the Enlightened." Siddhārtha Gautama (567-487 B.C.) was born in the Śākya tribe. His father, Śuddhodana, was the chief of that tribe. His mother, Māyādevi, died seven days after his birth. After that he was brought up at Kapilavastu by his stepmother Mahayapati, a sister of Mayadevi. He married Yashodhara and had a son, Rahula. Siddhārtha was living a prosperous and luxurious life. But he was not inwardly happy. The sights of an old person, a sick person, a corpse, and a peaceful and calm wandering monk impressed "emptiness of life" on his mind. He renounced the worldly life at the age of twenty-nine and became a wandering ascetic. After six years of severe ascetic practices and forty-nine days of deep meditation under a pipal tree at the outskirts of Gayā, he found the truth; found the secret of sorrow and suffering and understood the way to end it. He became "enlightened" (Buddha). He was then thirty-five years of age. After enlightenment, he preached "*dhamma*" for the next forty-five years, until his passing away (*parinibbāṇa*) at Kusināra at the age of eighty.

3.2. THE BUDDHA'S TEACHINGS

The Buddha gave his first sermon to five ascetics at the Deer Park, Sāranātha. This sermon is called "setting in motion the wheel of the religious law" (*dhamma cakka pavattana*). In this sermon, he explains the Four Noble Truths that he discovered in his enlightenment. These Truths are: suffering, the cause of suffering, the cessation of suffering, and the way to end the suffering (*dukkha, samudaya, nirodha, mārgga*). Suffering is understood in a very wide sense. It includes the real physical pain of old age, disease, and death; emotional pain, such as bereavement, minor irritations and dissatisfactions, the sense of not getting or losing good things and happiness which we want; the fear of getting things not wanted; and the passing of all things with the passage of time; the feeling of insecurity and there being nothing permanent to hold on to. This is the fact of suffering. The Buddha traces its cause to craving or thirst: the thirst for pleasure, the thirst for existence, and the thirst for prosperity. The third noble truth is the cessation of suffering. The fourth noble truth is that the noble eight-fold path leads to the cessation of suffering. It consists of right belief, right aspiration, right speech, right conduct, right means of livelihood, right endeavour, right memory, and right meditation. This eightfold path is reduced to wisdom (*pannā*), character (*śīla*) and equanimity (*samādhi*).

In his sermon, the Buddha also emphasizes the importance of avoiding two extremes:

A life given to pleasures and lusts: This is degrading, sensual, vulgar, ignoble and profitless; and a life given to mortifications: this is painful, ignoble and profitless. By avoiding these two extremes O Bhikkhus, the Tathagata has gained the knowledge of the Middle path (*madhyama patipada*) which leads to insight, which leads to wisdom, which conduces to calm, to knowledge, to the *sambodhi*, to *Nirvāṇa*.[6]

Jane Compson, in "Why Buddhism makes sense," writes: "The beauty of Buddhism is its simplicity. You need take nothing on authority, and metaphysical beliefs are not a prerequisite."[7] She adds:

What is attractive about this is not only its simplicity but the fact that it is so practical. It consists of a diagnosis and a course of action, which I can choose to follow if I want to. There is no concept of sin or damnation in Buddhism – it is a teaching on how to stop suffering which I can take or leave. Buddhism takes our everyday experience as its starting point and is therefore always "relevant" and pertinent to our lives.[8]

The Buddha preached religion without any revealed or speculative theology, cosmology or psychology, i.e. without propounding any theory, about God, Cosmos and soul: "To a Brahmin lost in philosophical truths about the eternity and the non-eternity of the world, Buddha says that he has nothing to do with theories. His system is not a darśana or a philosophy but a yāna or a vehicle, a practical method leading to liberation."[9] The Buddha anticipates someone saying "that he does not wish to lead the holy life under the Blessed one, unless the Blessed one first tells him whether the world is eternal or temporal, finite or infinite; whether the life principle is identical with the body or something differ-

---

[6] Ian S. Markham, ed., *A World Religions Reader* (Oxford: Blackwell, 1996), pp. 123-24.

[7] Ibid., p. 148.

[8] Ibid., p. 149.

[9] S. Radhakrishnan, *Indian Philosophy*, Vol. I, 2nd Ed. (London: George Allen and Unwin, 1956), p. 464.

ent, whether the Perfect One continues after death etc."[10] He compares such a person to a person

> pierced by a poisoned arrow and his friends, companions or near relations called in a surgeon, but that man should say: I will not have this arrow pulled out until I know, who the man is, that has wounded me; whether he is a noble, a prince, a citizen, or a servant; or whether he is tall or short or of medium height. Verily, such a man would die, ere he could adequately learn all this. Therefore, the man who seeks his own welfare, should pull out this arrow – this arrow of lamentation, pain and sorrow.[11]

The Buddha's attitude towards metaphysical problems is comparable to that of Kant. Kant argued that the existence of the soul, God, immortality, and freedom can be neither proved nor disproved by theoretical reason. He, therefore, concluded that these metaphysical problems lie outside the field of knowledge. He was an agnostic. But he thought that these beliefs were necessary for the possibility of morality. He therefore accepted them as "postulates of morality." The Buddha's attitude seems to be much more radical than that of Kant. Firstly, he did not hold that these beliefs are necessary for moral or religious life. Secondly, his silence on these metaphysical problems may be an expression of agnosticism but it is also interpreted as an expression of mysticism, pragmatism, or positivism.

Though the Buddha refused to answer ultimate metaphysical questions, he did provide a detailed causal account of the arising of suffering. By applying the Doctrine of Dependent Origination (*Paticca-samuppada*), he gives a series of twelve causal links: from ignorance spring formations of Karma; from them springs consciousness; from consciousness spring mind and body; from mind and body, the six senses; from the six senses arises contact; from contact arise sensations; from sensation, craving; from craving comes attachment; from attachment, "coming to be"; from "coming to be" arises birth; and from birth come old age and death."[12] By the destruction of the first (earlier) link, the chain of destruction of the next one continues.

Besides the four noble truths and the doctrine of twelve casual links, the Buddha is supposed to have taught three other fundamental truths. The basic ignorance which is the root cause of suffering is about these three fundamental truths. They are: (i) everything is transient, (ii) everything is soulless, and (iii) everything is full of sorrow (*sabbam aniccam, sabbam anattam, sabbam dukkham*).

---

[10] Ian S. Markham, ed., *A World Religions Reader* (Oxford: Blackwell, 1996), p. 125.

[11] Ibid., p. 125.

[12] A. L. Basham, *The Wonder that Was India* (Bombay: Rupa and Co., 1967), pp. 271-72; and S. Radhakrishnan, *Indian Philosophy*, Vol. I, 2nd Ed. (London: George Allen and Unwin, 1956), p. 410.

Normally we believe that things are stable. Even when changes are perceptible, as when a sprout grows into a tree, it is believed that underlying changes there is a stable, unchanging substance. A distinction is generally made between a permanent substance and changing qualities or states. The Buddha thinks that this is ignorance. Everything is flux. In this respect, there is much in common in the teachings of the Buddha, Heraclitus and David Hume. They take the flow of river-water or the burning flame as the paradigm of reality. Nobody can step into the same river-water twice, because by the time a person steps the second time, the water has already flowed. The flame appears to be steady and identical or the same at two time-instants, but it is constantly changing. This is true of everything in this universe. However stable and permanent an object may appear, it is undergoing constant changes, no matter how subtle and imperceptible they may be to our senses. What is called an object or a thing, therefore, is nothing but a series of states. There is no abiding unchanging substance underlying the series or changing states. What is regarded as the same and identical object underlying changes is therefore nothing more than similarities, resemblances, and causal links between successive states.

It is also believed that what is called a thing or an object is something simple that possesses qualities. Buddhism denies the existence of such a simple, single substance underlying plurality of qualities. It holds that everything is composite of qualities. Thus every object and every thing, however simple and abiding it may appear, is in reality composite and transient (*samghāta* and *santāna*). At the same time, a thing is merely an aggregate of states and qualities, and at different times, it is merely a succession of changing states and qualities.

This denial of one abiding substance underlying multiple changing states or qualities is equally applicable to the individual self. There is no permanent, simple abiding single soul-substance underlying the changing psycho-physical aggregate. This is called no-soul theory (*anattāvāda*). What is called the self, the "I," is an aggregate of five psycho-physical elements (*nāma-rūpa skandhas*). The four psychical elements are: sensations (*vedanā*), perception (*samjñā*), dispositions (*vāsanā*), consciousness (*vijñāna*), and the fifth element is bodily aggregate (*rūpa*). These five constantly vary in time and there is no permanent, simple soul-substance in an individual self. An individual is a continuous flow of changing physical and mental states from birth to death and there is no simple, abiding, identical soul underlying these changing states.

Thus every non-living thing and living being in this universe is an impermanent series of successive states without an underlying substance or soul. The universe is also a continuous flux. And the idea of permanence is a part of the basic ignorance which makes us seek and crave for permanence, and consequently makes life full of sorrow and suffering.

These doctrines, combined with the doctrines of karma and transmigration, provide the Buddhist account of the wheel of transmigration or becoming (*bhavacakka*). The Buddha's preaching of the middle path, which is the noble eightfold path, leads to wisdom (*pannā*), character (*śīla*), and equanimity and peace (*samādhi*). It leads to *sambodhi*, to *nirvāna*. This is the wheel of the religious law (*dhammacakka*). The religion (*dhamma*) preached by the Buddha is not only without God but is also without soul. The final state of *nibbāna* is not something that is caused or produced. If it were so, it would be impermanent and suffering. *Nibbāna* is only the destruction of the fire of lust, hatred, and ignorance, and consequent is cooling.

After the Buddha's passing away, all of his teachings were collected and arranged into three baskets by three councils. By the time of king Ashoka (273-236 B.C.) Buddhism was established as a distinct religion:

> Ashoka classified all the religions of his empire under five heads: the (Buddhist) Sangha, the Brahmans, the Ajivakas, the Nirgranthas (or Jainas) and "other sects." He further declared that, while he gave his chief patronage to the Buddhists, he honoured and respected them all, and called on his subjects to do likewise.[13]

> From the time of Ashoka, Buddhism began its outward march and by the seventh century A. D. had spread to Central Asia, China, Korea, Japan and Tibet in the North and to Ceylon, Burma Thailand, Cambodia, Vietnam, Malaya, and Indonesia to the south.[14]

Buddhism was divided into many sects and many schools of philosophy in India. It adapted itself to the environment and temperament of the people of the countries to which it went and gave rise to many sects and schools in them, as in India. It is beyond the scope of this paper to discuss these historical developments of Buddhism. We shall address the two main questions: What is the nature of humankind and its relation to external Nature in Buddhism? What is the Buddhist perspective on the role of technology in human development?

4. Veneration of Nature

(a) Jainism and Buddhism differ from each other on some basic philosophical tenets, and even hold opposite views. For example, according to Buddhism, the real is impermanent and changing, while Jainism regards the real as having origin, decay, and permanence. The real is permanent from the point of view of substance and impermanent from the point of view of modes. Jainism accepts the theory of soul-substance, while Buddhism holds a no-soul theory. Buddhism

---

[13] A. L. Basham, *The Wonder that Was India* (Bombay: Rupa and Co., 1967), p. 264.
[14] S. Radhakrishnan, ed., *The Cultural Heritage of India*, Vol. I, 2nd Ed. (Calcutta: Ramakrishna Mission Institute of Culture, 1993), p. 489.

regards earth, water, fire, and air as four material elements. For Jainism material atoms (*pudgala paramāṇus*) have no qualitative distinctions; they are all of the same type and earth, water, fire, and air are four types of immobile living beings.

According to Jainism the liberated soul goes to the place called *siddhaśīla* at the top on the border of occupied and unoccupied space, but for Buddhism the question, "Where does the bodhisattva go after death?" is as absurd as the question "Where does the flame go after it is blown out?"

(b) Despite these and similar differences in their basic tenets and religious practices, they speak almost with one voice about and have the same attitude towards nature and the role of technology in human development. Therefore, the Jaina and the Buddhist views on each of these issues will be discussed together in this and the next section.

Both Jainism and Buddhism hold that the human species is one among the many species of living beings. Like every other species, it has unique features. As the birds have the unique capacity to fly, and fish and other aquatic species to live in water, so humans have the capacity to preserve and transmit their knowledge through language from generation to generation, to practise morality and religion by taking vows, and so on. Animals, birds, and other non-human species do not possess this capacity. Both Jainism and Buddhism believe that human birth offers a unique opportunity to liberate consciousness from suffering and bondage, which opportunity, births in other species do not offer. But they do not hold that humans have sovereignty, control, or dominion status over other species and nature. They believe, on the contrary, in the equality of all living beings.

All living beings, including humans, are equal in so far as they share common concerns: "All beings love life. They wish to relish pleasures. They loathe pain. They abhor being killed. They are attached to this mortal coil. They want to hang on to life. Life is dear to all beings."[15] It would, therefore, be incorrect to say that the life of the strong is more valuable than that of the weak. All beings share in common a sense of insecurity and fear, sorrow and suffering, and dissatisfaction and lack of peace. Thus, despite differences in their capacities, physical structures, etc., they are all alike and equal in possessing common sentient nature and common concerns.

The bond between humans and other living beings becomes much more intimate in view of the belief that each one of us has undergone and will undergo many births in variety of species. Martine Batchelor writes, "When Buddhism travelled across Central Asia into China the vows of the Bodhisattva to help all beings were explained as the appropriate response to the fact that all beings

---

[15] Muni Mahendrakumar, trans., *Ayaro (Acaranga Sutra)* (New Delhi: Today and Tomorrow's Printers and Publishers, 1981), pp. 105-6.

have at one time or another been a parent to us."[16] In the Jaina scriptures also we find the argument for equality based on higher and lower births of the same individual:

> This self has many a time taken birth in higher clans or species as well as in lower ones. Therefore no being is low or high. No being has a special status. No being should crave for higher status. With this knowledge, who would accept differences or hierarchy in status? Who would be proud of one's own status? Who would hanker after a particular rank?[17]

Thus Buddhism and Jainism deny that humans have any special status in the universe; that all other living beings and nature are for human consumption; that humans can and should exploit the natural resources for their own progress and development. On the contrary, they are disturbed by the universal phenomenon of violence: "Beings torment other beings; there is great terror in this world. (As a result) beings are greatly tormented."[18] They, therefore, unhesitatingly prescribe the path of non-violence: "One should not injure, subjugate, enslave, torture or kill any animal, living being, organism or sentient being. This religion of non-violence is immaculate, immutable and eternal."[19] One must live in this world with minimum interference in the lives of other beings. One must recognise that the lives of other beings are as valuable as one's own life. They have intrinsic value and are not merely means to human welfare.

Both Jainism and Buddhism prescribe five precepts which form the minimum code of ethics for humanity to follow. They are called *panca-śīla* in Buddhism and *anuvratas* ("lesser vows") in Jainism. In Buddhism these precepts are: refrain from (a) harming living beings, (b) taking what is not given, (c) illegitimate sex behaviour, (d) false speech, and (e) taking intoxicants. In Jainism, the five vows are the same as Buddhism, except for the fifth one, which in Jainism is "refraining from acquisitiveness" in the place of "refraining from taking intoxicants." Following these precepts in daily life makes for self-restraint and non-exploitative, non-aggressive behaviour towards other living beings and nature.

Non-violence, the first precept, is understood so far in the negative sense of "not harming others." It only means "Live and let others live." But in view of the interdependence of living beings, non-violence means, "Live and help others live." Umāsvāti says, "[The function of] living beings is to render service to

---

[16] Martine Batchelor and Kerry Brown, eds., *Buddhism and Ecology* (London: Cassell, 1992), p. 6.

[17] Muni Mahendrakumar, trans., *Ayaro (Acaranga Sutra)* (New Delhi: Today and Tomorrow's Printers and Publishers, 1981), p. 102.

[18] Ibid., pp. 274-75.

[19] Ibid., pp. 183-84.

one another."[20] Living beings cannot live independently of each other. They affect each others' living. Therefore, they should cooperate and help each other to live a peaceful life. This implies that individuals cannot live thinking only of their own welfare and ignoring the welfare of others. So also humans cannot live thinking only about human welfare, because human welfare is a part and parcel of the welfare of all living beings and that of the planet earth.

This perception and understanding of the interrelatedness of the welfare of all living beings leads the eighth-century Buddhist poet Shantideva to talk of the organic unity of all living beings:

> In the same way as the hands and so forth
> Are regarded as limbs of the body
> Likewise, why are living beings
> Not regarded as limbs of life? [21]

According to this vision, humans, non-humans, and nature participate in the same cosmic life; they share in each others joys and sufferings. Both Jainism and Buddhism, therefore, recommend cultivation of the four types of feelings or attitudes towards all living beings and nature. They are "friendliness towards living beings, delight in the welfare of others, compassion for the miserable and lowly creatures and equanimity towards the vainglorious."[22]

The ideal of Bodhisattva is really a personification and embodiment of these four virtues. A bodhisattva who is concerned with the welfare of all beings and who makes the vow to save all beings, "dwells in friendliness, compassion, sympathetic joy and even-mindedness." The Buddha, describing how a disciple should cultivate loving-kindness (*metta*), says:

> And so with love for all the world
> Let him extend without bounds
> His heart, above, below, around
> Unchecked, with no ill will or hate
> Whether he stands or sits, or walks,
> Or lies (while yet not asleep)
> Let him such mindfulness pursue,
> This is Holy Abiding here, they say.[23]

---

[20] Umāsvāti, *Tattvartha Sutra (That Which Is)*, trans. Nathmal Tatia (San Francisco: Harper Collins, 1994), p. 131.

[21] Martine Batchelor and Kerry Brown, eds., *Buddhism and Ecology* (London: Cassell, 1992), p. 6.

[22] Umāsvāti, *Tattvārtha Sutra (That Which Is)*, trans. Nathmal Tatia (San Francisco: Harper Collins, 1994), p. 172; and Ashin Janakabhivamsa, *Abhidhamma in Daily Life*, trans. and ed. U Ko Lay, (Yangon, Myanmar: Ministry of Religious Affairs, 1997), pp. 99-111.

[23] Martine Batchelor and Kerry Brown, eds., *Buddhism and Ecology* (London: Cassell, 1992), p. 5.

Edward Cronze writes, "Friendliness consists in bestowing benefits on others; is based on the ability to see their pleasant side and results in stilling of ill-will and malice."[24] Compassion is participation in the sufferings and sympathetic joy in the happiness of others. Compassion is a virtue which uproots the wish to harm others. Sympathetic joy sees the prosperous condition of others, is glad about it, and shares their happiness. The attitude of impartiality or evenmindedness is directed towards all living beings who, in their ignorance, do not listen to the wise and follow a wrong path which is really baneful to themselves. One should not have anger or an attitude of condemnation towards such persons but should cultivate an attitude of "serene unconcern" or "equanimity."

According to Buddhism and Jainism, humans should not arrogate themselves as consumers, enjoyers, and users and treat everything else – living beings and natural resources – as mere objects for their consumption, enjoyment, and use; as merely means to their satisfaction. To think so is a false understanding and perverted vision about humankind's relationship with living beings and nature. As a matter of fact, humans are part and parcel of the animal world and nature and are dependent on them for their welfare. Humans cannot achieve their true welfare at the cost of the welfare of all living beings. They must, therefore, be animal-friendly, eco-friendly, and nature-friendly, and pursue human welfare in the context of the well-being of all living beings and the planet earth.

Let me conclude this discussion with a passage from a modern American Buddhist abbot, Ajahn Sumedho:

> Once you see what it is all about, you really want to be very careful about what you do and say. You can have no intention to live life at the expense of any other creature. One does not feel that one's life is so much more important than anyone else's. One begins to feel the freedom and the lightness in that harmony with nature rather than the heaviness of exploitation of nature for personal gain. When you open the mind to the truth, then you realize there is nothing to fear. What arises passes away, what is born dies, and is not self – so that our sense of being caught in an identity with this human body fades out. We don't see ourselves as some isolated, alienated entity lost in a mysterious and frightening universe. We don't feel overwhelmed by it, trying to find a little piece of it that we can grasp and feel safe with, because we feel at peace with it. Then we have merged with the Truth.[25]

---

[24] Edward Cronze, *Buddhist Thought in India* (Ann Arbor: University of Michigan Press, 1982), pp. 82-91.

[25] Martine Batchelor and Kerry Brown, eds., *Buddhism and Ecology* (London: Cassell, 1992), p. 15.

5. The Use of Nature and Human Development by Technology

We have so far seen how the Śramaṇa tradition in general and the Buddhist and Jaina religions in particular have conceptualized the relationship of humankind to the world of living beings and nature. Since humans are dependent on the animal kingdom and natural resources for their survival and development, they cannot avoid the use of other living beings and nature. They have to make use of agricultural, animal, and industrial products, and violence is involved in that process. Both religions, therefore, relax the rigour of non-violence in the case of lay persons. Jainism, for example, distinguishes between (i) intentional violence, (ii) violence involved in daily activities, (iii) violence involved in occupation and industry, and (iv) violence in self-defence.[26] Lay persons must abstain from the first type and reduce the violence of the other three types to the level of an unavoidable minimum. A lay person also has to choose occupations that involve less violence, e.g. trade, education, agriculture, etc. Buddhism does not allow its lay followers to choose the five occupations of trading in weapons, living things, meat, liquor, and poisons.[27] The general perspective of these two faiths on the use of nature is to use it with a minimum of violence, without doing much harm to the animal kingdom, plant life, and natural resources; to reduce violence to the unavoidable minimum level.

Even after taking all this care, one must be mindful of the fact, as the Korean Zen Master Ya Un points out, that

> From the time of ploughing and sowing until the food reaches your mouth and clothes your body, not only do men and oxen suffer great pains in producing them, but countless insects are also killed and injured. It is improper to benefit in this way from the hardships of others. Even more, how can you endure the thought that others have died in order that you can live?[28]

If we look at the use of technology from this perspective, it is permissible if and only to the extent that it does not increase violence. So technology which leads to high levels of pollution, which leads to large scale destruction of nature, which involves killing or torturing animals and other living beings, and which produces dangerous nuclear and chemical weapons would not be compatible with this perspective.

Another major objection to technology is that it empowers humans to enslave nature and the animal kingdom. This hampers the fundamental relationship of equality between humans, all other living beings, and nature. There is

---

[26] Muni Nyayavijayaji, *Jaina Darsana*, trans. Nagin J. Shah, *Jaina Philosophy and Religion* (Delhi: Motilal Banarsidass, 1998), p. 44-50.

[27] Martine Batchelor and Kerry Brown, eds., *Buddhism and Ecology* (London: Cassell, 1992), p. 7.

[28] Ibid., p. 8.

then no mutual relationship or give and take between them, no cooperation between them; but there is only one way coercion from humans to non-human nature; enslavement of nature by humans. As one modern author puts it:

> Man challenges nature; he harnesses it; he compels his will on wind and water; on mountain and woodland. The results are fantastic. But the price paid is very great. Things have been demeaned into objects. We have made ourselves lords of creation on the levels of utility and abstraction. We have compelled nature to yield knowledge and energy. But we have given to nature, that which is live and hidden within it, no patient hearing; no in-dwelling.[29]

In short such a technology has ravaged and devastated nature, instead of enriching it.

It may be argued that by the use of fertilisers, new technology, and bio-technology, humans have been able to yield high produce from agriculture and from animal resources, and thus have enriched human life. But it is forgotten that in the enthusiasm to yield quicker benefits, humans have caused degradation of land; the land has lost its natural fertility and has become almost barren in the absence of the use of fertilisers. So also cows have become milk-producing machines, hens egg producing machines, and goats and chickens are no more than food items. They have lost their intrinsic worth as living, sentient beings to be loved and cared for. In this process, humans have lost their sensitivity and have become greedy and calculative consumers. They have degraded themselves, both morally and spiritually, in so far as their treatment of nature and the animal kingdom is brutal and inhuman. Thus the whole mentality behind the aggressive use of technology is perverted. In running after sensuous pleasures, wealth, power, and luxuries, humans are ignoring inner peace, moral character, wisdom, and even spiritual virtues like friendliness, compassion, self-restraint, and so on. H. H. the Dalai Lama recognises that:

> Material progress is of course important for human advancement. In Tibet, we paid much too little attention to technological and economic development and today we realize that this was a mistake. At the same time, material development without spiritual development can also cause serious problems.... I believe both are important and must be developed side by side so as to achieve good balance between them.[30]

---

[29] George Steiner, *Heideggar*, 2nd Ed. (London: Fontana Press, 1992), p. 139.
[30] Martine Batchelor and Kerry Brown, eds., *Buddhism and Ecology* (London: Cassell, 1992), p. 111.

6. The Modern Relevance of Jainism and Buddhism.

We are living today on the threshold of a new age, not because it is the beginning of a new millennium of the common era, but mainly because unprecedented developments in science and technology have made the earth a global village and have brought to mankind new opportunities and new threats. We have reached a stage where secular and spiritual pursuits can no longer be separated. It is in this global and holistic context that the question of how different religious faiths look at mankind's relation with nature and the use of technology for human development becomes most pertinent and important.

It would be an anachronism to believe that Mahāvira and the Buddha in the sixth century B.C. were addressing themselves to the problems of ecological imbalance, environmental degradation, and the threat of nuclear weapons which we face today. The simple fact is that mankind did not face these issues at that time. But it would also be a grave error to think that what the ancients thought and said has no relevance for coping with today's challenges. I think the gravest predicament that mankind is facing today has three main aspects: (a) the limits and finitude of nature and the planet – e.g. the planet's fossil energy and non-renewable material reserves, its limited food-providing capacity and the question of climatic stability, its ability to sustain a growing human population load etc.; (b) the limits to mankind's technological power to dominate nature and to continue, improve, challenge, and surpass creation by human technology; and (c) what may be called "the inner limits" of mankind;[31] mankind's non-recognition of the need and reluctance and even refusal to bring about deep, inner, radical change in the human psyche, in its mind-set or mentality.

Thinkers are slowly realizing that, to solve the present crisis, what is required is not more technology but radical transformation of the human psyche:

> In the present ecocrisis humanity has to look for radical solutions. Pollution cannot be dealt with in the long term on a remedial or cosmetic basis or by tackling symptoms: all measures should deal with basic causes. These are determined largely by our values, priorities and choices. The human race must reappraise its value system.[32]

For bringing about this change in the human psyche, they are looking to the world religions.

It is really encouraging that many environmentalists, ecologists, welfare-activists, and philosophers all over the world, who are not committed to any religion, have begun to recognise the relevance of the world views, values, and

---

[31] Erwin Laszlo, *The Inner Limits of Mankind* (Oxford: Pergamon Press, 1978), pp. 1-4.

[32] Martine Batchelor and Kerry Brown, eds., *Buddhism and Ecology* (London: Cassell, 1992), pp. 28-29.

great teachings of the world religions in handling the present crisis. Similarly, many leaders of different religions are coming forward to reinterpret the religious truths and emphasise the universal aspects relevant to the psychological, socio-economic, political, environmental, and ecological issues we are facing today and to restrict the specific theological, cosmological, and eschatological doctrines to the followers of their own religious organizations. All these factors have led to mutual understanding, mutual respect, and mutual trust within the world community.

It is in this atmosphere of global understanding that I wish to end this paper by pointing out the modern relevance of the teachings of Jainism and Buddhism. Ervin Laszlo, while recognising the relevance of "the great ideals of the world religions," mentions the relevance of Judaism, Christianity, Islam, Hinduism, Confucianism, Taoism, and African tribal religions. He writes, "Buddhism too, perceives all reality as interdependent, and teaches man to achieve union with it through rejection of the drives and desires of a separate ego."[33]

Arne Naess, a leading deep ecosophist, says, "Buddhism provides a fitting background or context for deep ecology."[34] He suggests that it is necessary to develop a total view which recognizes that progress consists not merely or mainly in economic growth and high levels of consumption but in fulfilling the basic human needs like love and security, the welfare of all living beings on the planet, and saving the planet from destruction.

Lily de Silva brings out the relevance of the Buddhist teachings to our present crises:

> Buddhism offers humanity "the middle way," a simple moderate lifestyle eschewing both extremes of self-deprivation and self-indulgence. Satisfaction of basic human necessities, reduction of wants to the minimum, frugality and contentment are its important characteristics. Every individual has to order their life on moral principles, exercise self-control in the enjoyment of the senses, discharge their duties in their various social roles, and behave with wisdom and self-awareness in all activities. It is only when each person adopts a simple moderate lifestyle that humanity as a whole will stop polluting the environment. This seems to be the only way of overcoming the present ecocrisis and the problem of alienation.[35]

Michael Tobias, in *Life Force: The World of Jainism*, writes, "Jains were undoubtedly among the first people to focus upon this incantation, these basic

---

[33] Erwin Laszlo, *The Inner Limits of Mankind* (Oxford: Pergamon Press, 1978), p. 29.

[34] Michael Zimmerman, *et al.*, eds., *Environmental Philosophy: From Animal Rights to Radical Ecology* (Englewood Cliffs, New Jersey: Prentice Hall, 1993), p. 184.

[35] Martine Batchelor and Kerry Brown, eds., *Buddhism and Ecology* (London: Cassell, 1992), p. 29.

rights, this animal and planet liberation; upon the multi-faceted realm of what today we term environmentalism."[36]

It seems, therefore, that in our search for alternative philosophies or what Arne Naess calls "ecosophies," Jainism and Buddhism, the two representative religions belonging to the Śramaṇa tradition, have much to offer. Especially those who are not theologically and theistically inclined may find these two religions more attractive. Both advocate a life of self-restraint, austerities, and non-violence. Both recommend a non-aggressive, non-exploitative, and non-consumerist attitude towards all living beings and nature. Both recommend the cultivation of the attitudes of friendship and love, compassion and sympathetic joy, and impartiality to the whole world. Both use the metaphor of

a bee collecting nectar from flowers but not harming them in any way.[37]

According to the Sigalovada Sutta, a householder should accumulate wealth as a bee collects nectar from a flower. The bee harms neither the fragrance nor the beauty of the flower but gathers nectar to turn it into sweet honey. Similarly a human being is expected to make legitimate use of nature so that s/he can rise above nature and realize his or her innate spiritual potential.[38]

The Jaina scripture *Dasavaikalika Sūtra* also points out that a person should act like a bee. As a bee takes a small amount of nectar from each flower, without harming those flowers, and satisfies itself, so also a person who follows the religion of self-restraint, austerity, and non-violence should satisfy himself without harming nature.

Let me conclude this paper by mentioning the dream of H. H. Dalai Lama, the Nobel Peace Prize winner. He says, "It is my dream that the entire Tibetan plateau should become a free refuge where humanity and nature can live in peace and in harmonious balance."[39] He wants the Tibetan plateau to be "a zone of Ahimsa (non-violence) or Peace." Though this is a worthy dream, it is only a dream of a pilot project. The final dream that mankind must try to translate into actuality is to make this "global village" (the planet earth) the zone of peace in which all living beings live in harmony, peace, and prosperity.

---

[36] Michael Tobias, *Life Force: The World of Jainism* (Berkeley: Asian Humanities Press, 1991), p. 7.

[37] Martine Batchelor and Kerry Brown, eds., *Buddhism and Ecology* (London: Cassell, 1992), p. 80.

[38] Ibid., p. 22.

[39] Ibid., p. 112.

Appendix: The Jain cosmic time cycle, showing the two major divisions of half-cycles and further division into twelve aeons

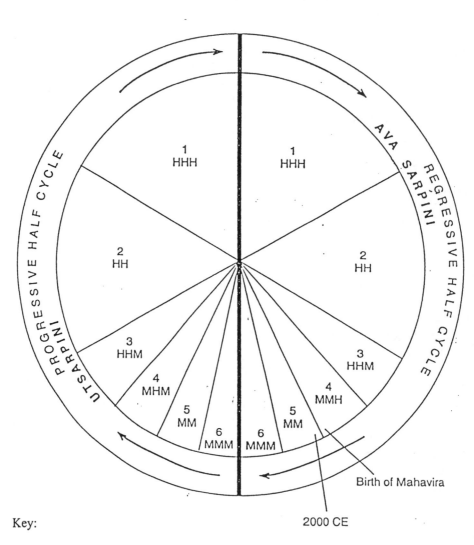

Key:

H = Happiness   M = Misery

1. Extremely happy	– HHH	–	very large period
2. Happy	– HH	–	very large period
3. More happy than unhappy	– HHM	–	large period
4. More unhappy than happy	– MMH	–	large period
5. Unhappy	– MM	–	21,000 years
6. Extremely unhappy	– MMM	–	21,000 years

DISCUSSION OF THE RELATIONSHIP TO NATURE AND TECHNOLOGY IN HINDUISM, BUDDHISM, AND JAINISM

Presentations:

D. P. CHATTOPADHYAYA:	Naturalism and Humanism in Creation and Construction in Hinduism
SHIVRAM S. ANTARKAR:	Veneration of Nature, Use of Nature, and Self-Improvement of Humankind by Technology in the Śramaṇa Tradition (Buddhism and Jainism)
Moderator:	ERNST ALBRECHT
Summary:	FRIEDRICH HERMANNI

1. The Status of Human Beings in the Cosmos

The status of the human person in the cosmos is assessed differently in the various religions. In the Western religions, the human person is regarded as the "crown of creation." In the Eastern religions, with the concept of rebirth, humans does not stand at the center of the cosmos. Nevertheless, there does seem to be a rank-ordering of living beings, since there can be either ascent or descent through karma. (ALBRECHT)

The difference between human beings and other living beings consists in freedom of action. In contrast to animals, who act only according to their instinct, humans can be held responsible for their actions. Humans are distinguished from other forms of live by this property, but are not higher than others. (ANTARKAR)

Because of their egoism, humans tend to classify themselves higher in the world than they actually are. This classification leads to isolation from the world and is not supported by the Indian religions. Human freedom as a distinguishing characteristic is assessed quite differently in Buddhism as well as in Hinduism and, therefore, is vague. Humans do not necessarily need to be assigned a definite position in the cosmos. (RAMAN)

P. Koslowski (eds), Nature and Technology in the World Religions, 121–124.

2. Nature and Non-Violence

ANTARKAR emphasized with reference to the theme of non-violence that this doctrine is never realized completely. Therefore, the requirement to be non-violent is not in effect for everyone, only for selected persons. But since the world is created in such a way that killing is necessary for survival (a fact which is the expression of the fallen world in Christianity) this requirement cannot be fully realized even by these special persons. The Buddhist or Jainist monk must at least kill plants in order to survive. (ALBRECHT)

Neither the Buddhist nor the Jainist monk would deny that life involves killing. The doctrine of non-violence is a maxim, an ideal, which can never be completely realized, since violence cannot be avoided, only minimized. There are different ways to come closer to the ideal. Some monks purify water before they drink it and wear a face mask to avoid killing small living beings. There is also a vow "to die without eating," which obligates one to refrain from eating as soon as one feels close to death. According to another doctrine, life forms with four, three, or two senses are never killed, only those with one sense, plants. The philosopher Canada, for example, ate only fruits and vegetables that had already fallen to the ground, in order to minimize killing. (ANTARKAR)

Doctrines such as these take non-violence too far. They resemble a kind of self-torture, which cannot be justified by religion. For this reason, many Buddhists are not vegetarians. (RAMAN)

Mahatma Gandhi pointed out that milk is not vegetarian, because it contains bacteria. The Jains declined this doctrine for pragmatic reasons. This attitude is reasonable, since non-violence is indeed an important doctrine, but should not be exaggerated. (ENGINEER)

The essence of the doctrine of non-violence is the change in awareness that comes with it. When someone becomes aware that he lives at the expense of other living beings, his attitude toward these other forms of live is changed. A person has a spiritually different life, when he does not think it is his right to be violent in order to live. (ANTARKAR)

Nature must not be considered the object of the human subject. Humans must instead always be aware that nature is also God's creation and that its special status consists in that. This is an attitude that avoids certain excesses that arise through the objectification of the world. (ALBRECHT)

3. The Morality of Technology

What does Buddhism have to say about the growth of the world's population? If more people live on the earth, will some type of technology be necessary to intervene in nature in order make it possible for everyone to live? But technology that intervenes in nature would be evaluated negatively by Buddhism. (Question from the audience)

Population grows because of technology. This is evaluated positively in Buddhism. Only technology that destroys life is regarded as bad. (ANTARKAR)

Since technology in itself is Janus-faced, this solution appears to be too simple. Every new discovery in medicine can also be used to kill people. Ultimately, human beings determines whether technology is good or bad. (ALBRECHT)

Technology in itself can be called neither good nor evil, since the purity of the motive is what determines the moral quality of its application. This criterion of evaluation is common to all religions. If technology is used wrongly, not the technology, but the person behind it must change. The person must be motivated by love of neighbor and compassion; only then will what he does be good for humanity. Religion promotes this spiritual attitude and supports people in performing good actions. (ANTARKAR)

One of the central problems of humanity is the fact that we attain more power through knowledge, but the moral quality of our actions does not improve. In this sense, our power appears unable to be responsible. (ALBRECHT)

4. Transmigration of the Soul

In response to a question from BRUMLIK about how he understood transmigration of the soul, ANTARKAR said that the question of how God created the world is also a secret, with which humans reach the limits of their powers of cognition and cannot know, but can only believe. Such a secret will be known only when one enters into it by faith, since the human mind cannot simply free itself from the conditioning of faith. Religion does not offer scientific concepts, only regulative ideas, which cannot be clarified by logic. Therefore, the theory of karma is just as much a mystery as the creation of the world or resurrection are mysteries. (ANTARKAR)

The personal identity of a soul requires memory. And a precondition of memory is the materiality of the soul. Is the soul understood to be material in Hinduism? (BRUMLIK)

The soul is always connected to matter. It has an astral or karmic body, in which all of a person's actions are unconsciously recorded. This karmic body is a part of the transmigrating soul. Even so, we cannot talk about a concrete memory. Having such a memory cannot be a precondition of rebirth, since chaos would ensue if the soul were to remember its previous lives. (ANTARKAR)

In response to the objection of ENGINEER that memory is necessary for the principle of reward and punishment, since otherwise it is not clear why someone should be rewarded or punished, ANTARKAR pointed out the distinction between the moral and the legal evaluation of action. Memory is necessary only for punishment in the legal sense. People know intuitively in view of their present lives what kind of actions they must have had. Beyond that, Jainism even formulates rules from which the causes of specific effects can be gauged. He himself considers the transmigration of the soul – analogously to the Christian idea of heaven and hell – as a purely regulative idea to encourage moral actions.

RAMAN agrees with BRUMLIK's statement that the concept of rebirth is not necessary for promoting environment-friendly behavior, since even without such an idea people must be aware that they are not permitted to maltreat animals, because of their ability to feel pain.

Koslowski pointed out at the conclusion of the discussion a crucial difference between Christian theology and the theory of rebirth: If one assumes rebirth, one behaves indifferently with respect to the present life. One lives with the belief that there are still many opportunities to obtain salvation in the future. In Christianity the requirement to act morally is strengthened by the fact that everyone has only *one* chance to be saved.

AN ATTEMPT TO SYNTHESISE FROM A HINDU PERSPECTIVE THE RECEIVED VIEW OF CREATION, THE RELATIONSHIP BETWEEN HUMANS AND NATURE, AND THE ROLE OF TECHNOLOGY

D. P. Chattopadhyaya

1. The Basic Structure of the Contributions on Buddhism, Islam, and Christianity

At the very beginning I must confess that there is no particular Hindu point of view from which I can try to synthesise the views represented by the learned contributors to the Third EXPO Discourse at Hanover during 22-23 June 2000. What I am attempting here is to organize their views from my point of view, which, one may feel, has its Hindu cultural underpinnings.

1.1. THE IDEA OF CREATION AND THE ETHICS OF THEISTIC AND ATHEISTIC RELIGIONS

The concept of Creation by itself does not seem to be problematic, unless we situate it in a religious context and view it in relation to the post-Darwinian scientific implications of evolutionism. If the traditional religious views of the relation between God and Creation/world are not basically contested, then the issues of human participation in the process of nature and the use of technology do not give rise to the kind of ethical problems that may deeply disturb moral and religious thinkers. The problems for religions like Jainism and Buddhism on the issues of the use of technology and environmental ethics, though otherwise very important, do not require the concept of God to be understood. In other words, a faithful Buddhist or Jain is perfectly entitled to speak about our admissible ways of using technology and ethical ways of entering into relationship with nature and non-human living beings.

Within the framework of Godless religions, not only the fundamental issues of human ethics, but also those of animal ethics and environmental ethics, make good sense. But it has to be admitted that all of these issues take on a different, problematic character when the notion of an all-knowing, all-good, all-pervasive, and all-powerful God is introduced. Additionally, it has to be recognized that the introduction of deistic, theistic, pantheistic, and panentheistic notions of

P. Koslowski (eds), Nature and Technology in the World Religions, 125–137.

God give rise to different kinds of ethical issues. The implied degrees of independence of humans from God or their dependence upon him entail various practical problems in the context of the admissible extent of technology in transforming nature.

1.2. COMMON FOCUS OF THE VEDIC, HINDU, BUDDHIST, AND JAIN RELIGIONS IN THE ETHICS OF KARMA

During the course of his enunciation of the principles of Buddhism and Jainism, Shivram S. Antarkar draws our attention to the highly ethical orientation of atheistic religions such as Buddhism and Jainism. To them, the theistic proofs of the existence of God – ontological, causal, teleological, etc. – hardly make any sense. Whether the world is deemed to be beginningless or eternal, they think, the question of its Creation does not arise. But they do recognize the importance of the Law of Karma, which means that humans are bound to reap the fruits of their actions; good actions bring good results, happiness, and even perfection, and bad actions lead to bad results. They do not believe in the principle of surrender to the will of God, because to them this is an empty concept. They emphasize the importance of right knowledge and right conduct, involving selfless work, self-control, and equanimity.

The *humanistic* accent of Jainism and Buddhism is unmistakable. The very words *Jina* (conqueror, self-conquest) and *Buddha* (enlightened) indicate that humans may be spiritually liberated through sustained ethical conduct and attain perfection enabling them to have the highest level of wisdom.

It may be recalled here that the historical Buddha was opposed to the Vedic authority and did not believe in Soul or God; yet he, in recognition of his spiritual enlightenment, has been accepted by Hindus as one of the ten incarnations of God (*Viṣṇu*, the Creator). In spite of the numerous differences between Vedic (Hindu) religions, on the one hand, and Jainism and Buddhism, on the other, their common emphasis on ethical conduct, right knowledge, and right action shows their religious affinity. Another point at which they seem to agree is respect for all forms of life, human and non-human, for all types of beings and things.

1.3. GOD'S WILL AND HUMAN FREEDOM OF TECHNOLOGY

In his professedly liberal interpretation of the Qur'an, Asghar Ali Engineer tries to show that there is no incompatibility between creationism and evolutionism. Although the traditional interpretation of the Qur'an does not seem to have left much room for human intervention in the process of Creation, it has been creatively interpreted by thinkers such as Iqbal, by utilizing the resources underlying the concept of *khalaqa*: the assistance of human beings (in the process of

Creation) suggests that they have a role to play, together with God, in sustaining it. The very fact that the Hazarat Mohammad brought about a fundamental social revolution in the Arabia of his time shows that exceptionally gifted individuals *can* facilitate God's own way of fashioning the direction of Creation. Extending this process of social engineering, it can be plausibly argued that biological engineering, cloning, and transplantation may also be viewed as permissible from the Islamic point of view, provided that they are in accord with, not contrary to, the spirit of God's own process of Creation.

Human beings, without ceasing to be human, i.e., finite, fallible and mortal, cannot know *exactly* the will of God, which is at work in the process of Creation. Consequently, human interpretations, even those given by the most learned persons or saints, are not found to be identical. That partly explains how even the most sacred texts of different religions, like the Vedas, the Qur'an, and the Bible, have lent themselves to different interpretations. For example, following the same Vedic authority, as many as six different philosophical systems and many more sub-systems have evolved in India. The same interpretative diversity is evident in almost all religions: Buddhism, Jainism, Christian, and Islam. That is why different sects and sub-sects are found within the fold of every religion. The plurality of interpretations and sects may justifiably be attributed to the emerging needs of time.

Of course, the strong determinist philosophers of religion believe that there can *be* nothing in this world, not even a slightest movement of a blade of grass, which is contrary to the will of God (expressed through laws). This deterministic interpretation implies, among other things, that freedom of the individual is practically free only to the extent that it is an articulation of God's own will. Whatever seems to be contrary to the will of God is, then, to be taken as a chimera/illusion.

This interpretation must meet the questions of evil and sin. Can humans *be* really sinners or evil-doers on their own account? Attempts have been made in many religious traditions to explain these "negative" phenomena in terms of an independent principle, independent of or other than God. The Principle of Darkness or Satan is at times cited as quite independent. In some other systems of religion these negative phenomena have been represented as "envelopment," "inversion," *not* negation, of God's will. If the sovereignty of God's will has to be defended in an *absolute* manner, humans can be granted mere "autonomy" or "freedom of will" only under the aspect of Divinity.

1.4. TECHNOLOGY AS PART OF THE PROCESS OF CREATION

Francis X. D'Sa attempts to show, following the principles of Christianity, how God as Creator and his Creation in the form of human beings can be shown to be mutually complementary. Through *continuous* Creation, God is said to be gradually and endlessly enlarging the scope of human freedom, lifting it from its narrow individualistic bounds.

The more humans can enlarge the scope of their freedom, the more they subscribe to God's process of continuous Creation. The same process makes their lives more meaningful and rich. There is no limit to the process of God's self-Creation in the world. This limitlessness of the process makes man more and more conscious of God's work in the world. Man can only facilitate this work, but cannot stop it.

Our understanding of the world, to start with, is perceptual, superficial, and therefore very limited in nature. At the same time, this perceptual process is ceaseless and bottomless. This character of the process makes us aware of the depth dimension of the world imparted to it by God.

The whole world is pulsated by God's presence in it. Our authentic self-realization requires us to be in union with this silent pulsation. This rhythm, though silent, is unstoppable. Many humans, under the dazzling impact of modern technology, think that the course of Creation designed by God can be swayed. Within the limited contexts of life, society, and nature our blinkered vision misleads us to believe that we can usurp, at least partially, the place of God in Creation. The Spirit of God that is at work in Creation knows no bounds and brushes aside our misguided attempts to reverse the course of continuous Creation. Rightly understood, God goes against only those who work against his process of Creation. Interestingly enough, the anti-human stance of God is *for* the benefit of human beings themselves. Their self-understanding and search for authentic being cannot be really blocked by a loving God.

If the defenders of science and technology can take a comprehensive view of the Creator and Creation, they can realize that there is no antagonism between what religion aims at and what technology is intended to deliver. Creation is God's gift to us and we humans, as the children of God, are expected to make use of technology in a way that is consistent with God's design. While technology addresses itself to the *specificity* of nature, religion situates the specificities within the *universal* design of God. Religion has nothing against technology until and unless it works contrary to the Spirit of God in Creation.

2. On the Presentation of Buddhism and Jainism by Shivram S. Antarkar

2.1. ATHEISTIC RELIGION

In Indian religious thought two different religious traditions – Brahmanic (or Vedic) and Śramaṇic – are very notable for more than one reason. The Brahmanic one is essentially Vedic, accepts the infallibility of the Vedic authority, and is theistic or pantheistic in nature. The Śramaṇic tradition questions the authority of the Vedas, rejects the idea of God as supreme reality, and yet proclaims itself as a religion or *dharma* (Sanskrit) or *dhamma* (Prakrit).

First, in the world-outlook of the Śramaṇa tradition, God has no place. Therefore, its cosmology is not God-based. It rejects the received theistic proofs for the existence of God: ontological, causal, cosmological, and teleological. The question of proving the non-existence of God does not make sense to the Śramaṇa.

Second, if God is found to be non-existent, the question of taking him as an infallible source of knowledge does not arise at all. Whether the world is deemed to be beginningless or eternal, the question of its Creation does not arise. When the spiritual potentiality of man is fully realized, he becomes all-knowing and his knowledge unquestionable. On the basis of his all-knowing character, he is able to draw the distinction between the right and the wrong, between the good and the bad.

Third, having dispensed with the idea of God, this Śramaṇa tradition feels the ethical necessity of accepting the Law of Karma to ensure good fruits for the good actions and bad fruits for the bad actions of human agents.

Fourth and finally, the Vedic tradition advocates the ideal of total surrender to the Will of God as a means to the attainment of salvation. The Śramaṇa tradition emphasizes the importance of right knowledge and right conduct for achieving liberation. It may be added here that in both the Vedic and the Śramaṇic traditions the importance of knowledge, surrender, and ethical conduct have received recognition in different ways.

The Śramaṇa tradition is said to be as old as, if not older than, the Vedic one. The idea of Śramaṇa has been defined in terms of three main concepts, effort (*śrama*), control (*dama*), and equality/equanimity (*sama*). This tradition is marked by strong spiritual individualism. It includes many sects. The main two sects that gained great prominence and historically have long endured are Buddhism, associated with the name of Gautama Buddha, and Jainism, associated with the name of Vardhamāna Mahāvīra. It is interesting to note that both Buddha and Mahāvīra hailed from aristocratic backgrounds and belonged by birth to the warrior-administrator (*kṣatriya*) caste. They were contemporaries (c. 600 B.C.) and lived and preached in more or less the same eastern areas of India.

2.2. TRANSFORMATION OF GROSS INTO SUBTLE KARMA-MATTER

The word *Jaina* is derived from the root *jina* (conqueror). He who follows the path of *jina* is known as Jaina. A true Jaina is venerable, fights the wrongdoer, overcomes the cravings of the flesh, and follows the teachings of his enlightened predecessors. Mahāvīra, the founder of Jaina religion, is said to have been preceded by twenty-three tirthankaras (spiritual preceptors). This suggests that Mahāvīra had a long tradition behind him.

In Jaina ontology the main two categories are living (*jīva*) and non-living beings. The living beings are characterized by their mobility, sense-organs, and birth. Earth, water, fire, air and vegetation, insects, birds, animals, etc. are endowed with living characteristics in varying degrees. In contrast, the non-living beings are of five types: matter, medium of motion, medium of rest, space, and time. Matter is of two forms: atomic and aggregative. Atomic matter is uncreated and eternal. Aggregative matter is of several levels, gross and subtle. Some of the aggregative bodies are credited with living properties, the capacity to breath, speech, and mind. The most subtly body is karmic – due to action (karma). This subtle body can move from one life to another. The Jaina thinkers use the word *jina* to denote both the liberated souls and the empirical ones in bondage. The liberated souls have infinite knowledge, infinite power, and perfect character. The souls in bondage, however, are subject to various limitations and are bound to the chain of birth and death. Jainism speaks of two requirements for the release of the empirical souls: (i) stopping the inflow of action-related (karmic) matter and (ii) shedding the load of past karma (action). When the soul is completely cleansed of the effects of all past karmas, it attains pure and omniscient (*kaivalya*) character. Even after attaining this high stage, the soul can perform certain actions without inviting the inflow of bonding effects. It is a life of purity, austerity, meditation, and contemplation.

In the face of it, the framework of Jaina ontology is taxonomic, conceptual, and static. This sort of ontology, which internalises dynamic elements within it, is not peculiar to Jainism. Enumerating the basic categories of being and relating them to one another have been accepted as philosophy and religion by many other systems of the East and West. Jaina faith is not only ethical. Its religious content, as is evident from its emphasis on liberation, respect for all forms of life, and spiritual disposition, is very comprehensive and rich.

2.3. THE EIGHTFOLD PATH OF FREEDOM AND THE TWELVE LINKS OF THE CAUSAL CHAIN

No major religion of the world appeared and was able to become popular with the people suddenly. Buddhism, like Jainism, had its cultural and spiritual ancestry mainly among the peoples of eastern India and the Himalayan foothills. The recognized founders of religions assimilate their past values, and prove themselves acceptable and adorable to their people, because of their high spiritual attainment, charismatic personality, exceptional courage, sacrifice, and communicative competence.

Siddhārtha (567-487 B.C.) was born in a princely family of the Śākya tribe. Trained to be kind, he married and had a son. But before he could settle down to an ordinary household life of comfort and affluence, he began to feel a deep spiritual discontent within himself. Different forms of human suffering – disease, old age, death, and grief – led him to reflect on their causes and the possible ways of removing them. In search of light and truth about these essential questions, he left behind the family life and kingdom and wandered from land to land. After prolonged meditation under a Pippal tree near Gaya, he found the light and became enlightened (Buddha). Siddhārtha became Buddha and realized the Four Noble Truths: (i) there is suffering; (ii) there is a cause of suffering; (iii) that cause can be known and (iv) removed. Desire is the root cause of suffering. Freedom from desire must be aimed at and attained. The path of freedom from suffering passes through (a) right belief, (b) right aspiration, (c) right speech, (d) right conduct, (e) right means of livelihood, (f) right endeavour, (g) right memory, and (h) right meditation.

Buddha's emphasis on practice and aversion to theoretical speculation leads Antarkar to liken him to Kant. While for Kant, God, the Immortality of the Soul, and Freedom are postulates, Buddha refuses to speculate on these metaphysical issues beyond the bounds of human experience. His agnosticism and mysticism are earth-bound and practice-oriented. The main principle that shows his worldview's close linkage with our everyday experience is that of Dependent Origination. In brief, it says that there is no *causa sui*, i.e., every cause has its cause and there is no absolute cause. The causal chain is long and has numerous – as many as twelve – links: (1) ignorance gives rise to (2) action, from action (3) consciousness, (4) mind-body, (5) six senses, (6) contact, (7) sensations, (8) craving, (9) attachment, (10) "to be," (11) birth, (12) growth, decay, and death. None of these links or stages is ensouled, permanent, and free from sorrow. Everything, every being is in the nature of a flux.

The Buddhist does not believe in the substantive nature of anything. To him, every seemingly substantive thing is an aggregation of passing states. The soul of man is no exception to this general principle. It is an aggregate (*skandha*) of names and forms (*nāma-rūpa*) of five different psycho-physical elements. The account of self-identity given by Buddhism is thoroughly phenomenalist. No-selfism (or *nairātmyavāda*) is a basic tenet of Buddhism. An individual, strictly speaking, is said to be a series of states, a flow or flux. Every psycho-physical state has its own alternative ways of constructing or imaging "its" past states. Backed by the tenets of karma and transmigration, the life of every individual is chained to the wheel of the empirical world. But following the eightfold middle path of dharma (religion) one can attain nirvāṇa (liberation), can be free from all desires – after-effects of and impulses towards actions. Nirvāṇa is like a blown-out lamp: it is indescribable.

Within a couple of centuries of Buddha's nirvāṇa, his message reached distant countries of South-East Asia and the Far East. It is perhaps the only one of the major world religions that did not have to depend in the least on political patronage and power in order to spread far and wide. Antarkar attempts to show that both Buddhism and Jainism had in their teachings something so valuable and universal that it won over the hearts of innumerable people of different countries. First, the founders of these two religions stressed the equality of all living beings, human and non-human, without according a privileged status to the human species. Secondly, they highlighted an all-pervasive sense of insecurity, born of suffering and peacelessness, in all beings, leading them to yearn for peace, love, and harmony with all living beings and things. Their commitment to peace and non-violence made their basic message clear to all humans, irrespective of their ethnic roots, geographical location, cultural and local religious ancestry.

So that the ideal of human unity may be realized, Buddhism recognises five basic moral maxims: (i) not to hurt any living being, (ii) not to take what is not given, (iii) to shun illegitimate sexual behaviour, (iv) not to indulge into falsity, and (v) not to take any intoxicant. In addition to these moral maxims, Jainism preaches an additional principle: non-possessiveness. The upshot of this principle is intended to induce human beings to love nature, to be cooperative in character, to be non-violently disposed toward all living creatures, and to be eco-friendly. Buddhism and Jainism require humans to be concerned with others' welfare and not to indulge in consumerism. At the same time these religions encourage fearlessness and heroism.

The Śramaṇa tradition in general, and Buddhism and Jainism in particular, emphasize the importance of non-violence. At the same time, they recognize its unavoidability in practical life. Therefore, they advise us to follow the path of minimum violence. Violence in defence and in unavoidable occupations and industries is allowed. Occupations entailing patent violence, viz., trading in weaponry, living creatures, meat, liquor, and poisons, are prohibited for the followers of Buddhism.

2.4. SANCTITY OF NATURE

Buddhism and Jainism are not opposed to technology as such. In fact, civilization itself involves and makes use of various technologies, such as agriculture, house-building, cooking, and making medicines to cure diseases. Only those forms of technology that violate the principles of non-violence, eco-friendliness, or harmony with other beings and things are prohibited. As a corollary of these maxims, man is expected to refrain from land-degrading and water- and air-polluting technologies.

Antarkar rightly points out that the basic principles of Buddhism and Jainism are not only compatible with, but also promotive of, human needs in the modern age. Since natural resources are limited in supply, humans are expected to use them in a judicious manner. Nature should be treated as a sustainer (like a mother) and not merely as an object of exploitation and consumption. The sacredness of nature should be evident in our modes of interaction with it. Unless we can control our own inner impulses, our attitude toward nature cannot be ecosophic. Once the interdependence of nature and culture, things and beings, is deeply realized, we are likely to be both austere and loving in our disposition. Wisdom is lodged not only in our spirit but also in our body. Once that wisdom is rightly realized, our use of technology and our interaction with nature are bound to be peaceful and harmonious.

3. Francis X. D'Sa on the World as Creation and Creation as a Cosmotheandric Reality

3.1. RELATIONSHIP OF CREATOR AND CREATURE INSTEAD OF SUBJECT AND OBJECT

In every religion one finds some account of God, the world, and the human person, as well as attempts to define their relation. Francis X. D'Sa tries to understand the relation from two points of view: that of faith and that of belief. Belief is rated above faith, because of its proclaimed reflective character.

D'Sa offers his interpretation of the Christian beliefs about Creation. Reflection convinces him that the Semitic account of the relation between Creator and Creation, marked by dichotomy, is unfounded. This distinction should not be likened to the epistemological distinction between Subject and Object. On the contrary, the Creator is inherent in his Creation. In fact, Creation is continuously and effectively informed of the power and wisdom of the Creator. Our reflection makes us aware of our limitation, and also our dependence on the Creator. In the name of *free* self-understanding, man should not be individualist, self-centric, and oblivious of the Creator in all spheres of his Creation.

When we rise above our narrow individualism and, on reflection, become conscious of our true nature, we feel not only dependent upon God, but we ourselves, human beings, realize our inter-dependence, belonging to God in our togetherness. God in his infinite goodness has *not* subdued any part of his Creation, human or natural, to his will. His character of *continuous* Creation, his effective presence in history, is designed to improve the whole of Creation, everything human and everything natural. The continuous and creative presence of God in Creation makes the world-history non-linear and richly complex. God is always actively creative in his Creation for the benefit of its Creatures.

3.2. FOR A TECHNOLOGY IN THE ONTONOMIC LAW OF CREATION

Creation is a part of the self-understanding of human beings. The true self-understanding of man makes him conscious of the law of his being at work in the world. This law has been said by Panikkar to be ontonomic. This law is expressive of the many-sided and harmonious relationship of the things of the world. This law manifests God's presence and work in the world.

Reflection on God's work in the world reveals several things. Firstly, we become convinced that the world created by God defies our attempts to manipulate its process. We can change the course of nature only marginally, but not fundamentally. We are neither author of nature nor of ourselves. Secondly, the world that has been *given* to us needs to be nurtured by us. We have a religious *obligation* to follow the laws of the world and to be increasingly conscious of its complexity and *limitlessness*. Finally, our true relation with Creation as a part of it is to work *for* it and not *against* it.

In the modern age dominated by reason and technology, many of us are inclined to forget the inner Spirit of technology. Ultra-rationalism, leading to the abuse of reason and science, tends to make us oblivious of the Spirit of reason. Spiritually informed science and technology find no ground of conflict with the Creation of God. Spirit is always informed of the harmonic whole, the wholeness of reality. The entire realm of Spirit is never exhaustibly accessible to our limited reach of perception. When man is blindly faithful to the dictates of perception, he misses the voice and call of Spirit. Only a holistic or integral realization of Creation helps us to see the correct perspective of the relation between religion and technology.

While religion drives us to the search for the true *meaning of life*, it does not, or rather cannot, make us blind to the attending difficulties of that process of search. Technology is basically concerned with practical problems which beset us in our search for the *authentic meaning* of life, living, and salvation. When the Spirit of religion is brought to bear upon the workings of technology, the latter assume their human character and discloses its Spiritual orientation.

3.3. OPENING UP RELIGION TOWARDS TECHNOLOGY AND TECHNOLOGY TOWARDS RELIGION

When, in the context of technology and science, we speak of spirituality, one may feel disturbed. But once we realize the true import of a "cosmotheandric" vision of reality, to use an expression of Panikkar, we will be able to see the correct relation between (a) what is *perceptible*, (b) what is *perceiving*, and (c) the *depth-dimension* of the reality. We must free our mind from the narrow realm of phenomenalism. Beyond perceived phenomena there is a vast realm. Perception itself gives glimpses of that realm. Beneath, behind, and beyond sense-perception there lies the depth-dimension of reality. These three dimensions are not mutually exclusive, but verily inter-penetrative.

Once the dimensional specificity as well as the holistic integrality of Creation are properly understood, the fancied conflict between science and technology, on the one hand, and religion and spirituality, on the other, begins to disappear. Only then does the one-sidedness of reason melt down and the cosmic vision dawn upon us. Technology certainly has its use. It enables us to enlarge our epistemic reach. Science and its laws provide us insights into the nature of reality, both microscopic and macroscopic. But D'Sa attempts to show that technology is interested only in a few human beings and does not appear to be concerned with the larger issues, such as peace, justice, equal opportunities, and welfare for all.

In contrast, religion, being busy as it is with the larger and deeper issues of life, seems to be indifferent to what happens in the field of technology. But this is not in accord with the true spirit of religion, which is all-comprehensive. Neither religion nor technology is expected to be one-sided. Only in their togetherness, through their integral approach, can we have a cosmic religious vision of the world. This vision leaves behind narrow individualism and rejects dualism. In their joint enterprise, technology must be depth-oriented and religion practice-oriented. Religion, in its preoccupation with the cosmic vision of the world and its depth-dimension, must not neglect the specifics of our practical life.

3.4. CONSERVATION OF CREATION AS A TASK OF GRATITUDE

To be a believer in the true sense is to realize the presence of God in the world and what he has given to us. The gift of God in the forms of natural resources and environmental beauty binds us to God as giver. Our vision of God and our gratitude to him are not based on his technocratic skill of creation, but on his abundance of love for and sustenance of all that he has created.

We should not try to understand the nature of creation in a piecemeal way, but instead in a holistic fashion. The many views and values which are available in the world should all be taken into account, even if these are not equally acceptable on their merits. Humans are called upon by the godliness of creation, not only to be tolerant of differing views, but also to be respectful towards the same.

As an expression of our gratitude to God we must do everything possible for us to sustain the purity of nature, without polluting or exploiting it in the least. Both religion and technology are expected to be promotive of the spirit of human cooperation, if not identification, with the developmental impulse lodged in the bosom of nature.

4. Islam's View of Humankind's Relationship with Nature and Participation in the Process of Creation with the Help of Technology according to Asghar Ali Engineer

4.1. CREATION, HUMAN BEINGS, AND NATURE

Asghar Ali Engineer, by his liberal interpretation of the Qur'an, tries to narrow down the alleged difference between creationism and (pro-Darwinian) evolutionism. He finds no contradiction between Creation (attributed to the Will of God) and evolution, which may be construed both as an autonomous natural process and also in relation to human partnership with it. To him these concepts, rightly understood, are complementary, not contradictory. Pre-human and independent nature is easily conceivable but the emergence and existence of human phenomenon without nature seems to be inconceivable.

4.2. WHAT IS THE ISLAMIC POINT OF VIEW?

There is no unique Islamic view on the relation between Creation and evolution. The orthodox view, derived from the Qur'an, does not accord any place to evolution within the process of Creation. But many interpreters, particularly the modern ones, recognise the place of evolution in the concept of Creation. The very revolutionary socio-politico change brought about by the Prophet himself in Arabia is often cited as a supporting evidence. What the Arabic people achieved under his leadership was indeed revolutionary. It was more than mere evolution. Some interpreters, such as Muhammad Ali and Iqbal, tried to show that God in his creative acts may go on entirely by himself (*ibda*) or make use of physical categories like space and time, and accept the assistance of human beings (*khalaqa*).

God is both creator and sustainer (*rabb*) of the world. The process of sustenance implies the existence and continuation of the world of living beings. The merciful and compassionate God accepts human assistance in realizing his high aim of Creation. Unaided by materials and tools, finite and fallible human beings cannot effectively participate in Allah's process of creating the best possible world.

It is in this context that Engineer introduces the role of technology, to be used by man in improving the quality of Creation. God's gift of man's creative intellect is also intended to facilitate the process of evolution within the scheme of Creation. Human intellect, endowed with the power of discernment, can well distinguish between good and bad, between right and wrong, and act accordingly. To sustain the process of Creation, due to Allah, man is required to make good use of his intellect and technology. In addition, he is expected to take good care of natural resources and utilize and distribute them properly.

4.3. CLONING AND TRANSPLANTATION

Through the developmental process of technology, new horizons of Creation are now clearly visible. In addition to natural sustenance and biological development, human technology has added new chapters to the Creation of life. Cloning and transplantation bring out this hitherto unexplored potentiality of nature. Biological engineering need not necessarily be construed as anti-Islamic. If biological engineering, like social engineering, is in accord with Allah's Will itself to sustain and develop the human species, then there is nothing wrong in it. After all, if human assistance facilitates Allah's own process of Creation, it is to be accepted as Islamic, not prohibited by Islam.

4.4. AN ETHICAL QUESTION

Technological development raises some ethical questions. The critic may question the advisability of using radical technological development such as cloning. Simply because it is scientifically possible, it has been asked, should we go for it, interfering with the Will of God? From an *enlightened* Islamic point of view, the question may be answered in this way: Whatever benefits human beings, reduces their chance of deformity and disease, should not be prohibited. In extreme exigency, even what is ordinarily prohibited has been allowed by the authoritative interpreters of the Qur'an. What helps and sustains humans seems to have the blessings and approval of Allah.

4.5. THE ISLAMIC POINT OF VIEW REITERATED

In order to solve or dissolve controversial ethical question, no great religious leader has ever come forward with a single view or principle. Interpretative plurality is a transparent historical reality. It would be wrong to suppose that all Islamic believers will subscribe to a unique interpretation or solution as the only plausible one. The fact that a particular technology, whether social or biological, may be abused by a few misguided persons is not grounds for its ethical prohibition. The bad use of a good thing is not an argument against its good and better uses.

Human beings in general, and enlightened ones in particular, are called upon to reflect on the basic truths enunciated by the Prophet in the Qur'an and its wise interpreters in the light of unfolding needs of the time and human beings.

CONCLUDING DISCUSSION OF THE RELATIONSHIP TO NATURE AND THE INTERPRETATION OF TECHNOLOGY IN THE WORLD RELIGIONS

Moderator: PETER KOSLOWSKI

Summary: FRIEDRICH HERMANNI

In his synthesis CHATTOPADHYAYA did not so much emphasize the contradictions between the religions as neutralize them. Max Weber asserted that in an Asian tradition one understands oneself as a vessel of God that receives everything into itself, while in a Western tradition one sees oneself as a tool, as an acting instrument of God. This contradiction is missing from the synthesis. (BRUMLIK)

A bigger difference between Eastern and Western religions is the way in which they attempt to achieve a transformation of the human soul. Human consciousness is at first self-centered and egoistic, and it is the goal of religion to liberate the soul from this self-centeredness. This can happen in two ways. In the theistic way, egocentrism is overcome by "theo-centrism." One subordinates oneself to God and understands oneself to be his instrument. In the non-theistic way, one does not overcome egoism by God, but instead by regarding oneself as a spiritual being who is in the position to overcome oneself by changing direction toward that of another being. (ANTARKAR)

ENGINEER pointed out in this context that religious leaders do not represent a religion. If they attain a higher state of consciousness, that does not yet have anything to do with the consciousness of the masses. For the masses, subordinating oneself to God only means submitting to moral laws.

The theory of evolution seems to be a special challenge for the religions. It maintains that everything that we can do and know and are is the product of a blind process, controlled by accidents and devoid of higher meaning. Therefore, this world view maintains a "higher meaninglessness" of human history, which appears to be incompatible with the religions. (BRUMLIK)

There is no fundamental distinction between divine creation and divine evolution. Creation should not be seen as the final "version" of the world. Both theological assertions and empirical data must be interpreted, and such an interpretation is always conditioned by a non-static, dynamic culture. (ENGINEER)

P. Koslowski (eds), Nature and Technology in the World Religions, 138–139.

BRUMLIK supposes and ANTARKAR agrees that the Asian religions are more compatible than Western religions with the theory of evolution, because they do not see the human race as the crown of creation.

The contradiction between the scientific and the religious model of evolution does not exist per se, but instead only originates from the question "creation *or* evolution?" In order to answer this question, one must take into consideration that it involves positions with different standings within their respective models. The theory of evolution is a weak point of modern science, since it cannot unite all of the results of genetics with itself. Creation, on the contrary, is an idea that is often understood incorrectly. Neither the idea of evolution nor belief in creation is defended by the best intellectuals. Beyond that, there is much room for interpretation in what the Bible and the Qur'an say about creation. The "Big Bang" could be interpreted as an act of creation. (HORUZHY)

According to Hinduism, God created the world out of different substances. In what ways does modern philosophy in India attempt to produce a unity of nature, God, and man? (MUHAMMAD SHAMA)

The Vedānta achieves this unity by the concept of Brahman ("World Soul," God). This is a universal principle and says that human beings and nature are only the expression of Brahman. (ANTARKAR)

Many people seek a redefinition of the relationship with nature, because Western civilization has reach the point of a crisis, in which our common necessities of life are threatened. There are two possibilities ways to achieve such a redefinition: via an enlargement of human awareness and via normative restraints on human action, such as "Life is holy." In a secularized world, however, the latter way would lead to the question: "Why should life be holy?" That would only lead to an enlightened anthropocentrism, which maintains that life must be holy, because otherwise the human race would destroy itself. Can one interpret the Jain tradition to mean that the interests of humans should be safeguarded ahead of reverence for other forms of life, or do the interests of these other life forms really come first? (Question from the audience)

The Jain tradition does not advocate this form of anthropocentrism, but instead hallows the other forms of life independently of the interests of humans, and thus advocates biocentrism. (ANTARKAR)

The confrontation of Western and Eastern thought traditions does not help to solve contemporary problems in world politics, since by now the so-called Western thought model is everywhere. Western thought about technology can amalgamate itself with different religions. Therefore, a new view of nature is needed. This can be achieved only if each person becomes aware of his or her own religious tradition. What is being sought in the Eastern religions can just as well be found in the biblical religions, if one is liberated from the prejudice that it is the biblical tradition that has been the essential motor for the technological subjugation of the world. (BRUMLIK)

CONVERSATION BETWEEN THE REPRESENTATIVES OF THE WORLD RELIGIONS AFTER THE CONCLUSION OF THE PUBLIC DISCOURSE

Moderator: PETER KOSLOWSKI

Summary: FRIEDRICH HERMANNI

1. Is there in the world religions a common denominator and a shared view of what makes a religion a religion?

Three characteristics appear to be common to all religions: The center point of a religion is its mythology. In addition, it must be the foundation for social organization. Finally, the external form of a religion is shaped by art and its symbols, paintings, architecture, dance, and music. (RAMAN)

Islam has no mythology. The term for religion in Islam is *din* (law). Islam is a law-centered religion and the *Shari'a* (Islamic law) plays a central role, since the purpose of the religion is to regulate human life and to lead people to Allah. The literal meaning of "Islam," on the other hand, is two-fold: First, it means to subjugate oneself to the will of God. Since one of God's names is "Salam" (peace), subjugating oneself to God also means subjugating oneself to peace. That is the essence of religion in Islam. (ENGINEER)

In order to answer the question about the commonalities of the world religions, it is incorrect to compare their external features. One must instead ask about their functions and the function of religion in general. If the function is reduced to the regulation of human life, and therefore to morality, that raises the question whether there is anything at all that goes beyond this worldly ethic. (ANTARKAR)

It seems helpful for answering the question of the essential features of a religion to differentiate religion from philosophy. Because the interest of this discourse is philosophical, it is not so easy to distinguish between philosophy and religion, as one can see in the case of Buddhism. Is there a difference between Buddhist philosophy and Buddhist religion? (KOSLOWSKI)

The goal of Buddhism is *nirvāna* or *mokṣa*, the liberation of human consciousness from materiality, and can be considered in analogy to Christian redemption. This concept goes beyond a pure worldly ethic, and in this sense is

P. Koslowski (eds), Nature and Technology in the World Religions, 140–145.
© 2001 *Kluwer Academic Publishers. Printed in the Netherlands.*

religious. (ANTARKAR)

Is redemption or salvation a central point of every religion, and therefore an essential characteristic of religion? (KOSLOWSKI)

It is possible that the idea of redemption is common to all religions. But it is not specifically religious, and can also be a part of a philosophical system. Moreover, this discussion should not be about individual aspects, since not every individual aspect within a religion is taken into consideration and not every individual aspect of the respective religions is represented. (IDEL)

Religions that start out from redemption are very exclusive. Furthermore, redemption is a different concept from *nirvāna* or *mokṣa* and has a different history. When such concepts are reduced so much that they can be equated, one no longer does justice to them. Religion is essentially man's search for meaning. That seems to be a common denominator and must be investigated more closely. (D'SA)

In reply to the objection that this is also true of philosophy, D'SA emphasized that he makes no distinction between philosophy and religion.

To deal with religion in a philosophical horizon means to take account of the ontology, the "situation of being" upon which it is based. The basic principle of religion is that the entirety of reality is not reduced to empirical existence, but instead another mode of being is included. Therefore, religion postulates another mode of being and, from this perspective, redemption appears to be a way of concretizing our horizon on another mode of being. (HORUZHY)

Nevertheless, religion is a concrete entity and has a social strategy. This must be taken into consideration, since otherwise systems will be discussed that are indeed fascinating, but are merely systems, not religions. (IDEL)

There is no contradiction here. IDEL is talking about religion as a collective phenomenon. Of course, religion includes social aspects. The postulation of another mode of being, on the contrary, is the description of the religious attitude. (HORUZHY)

The symbolic character of religion must not be passed over. It is an essential mark of religion. (RAMAN)

HORUZHY responded that the symbolic character is not the primary characteristic of religion, only a secondary feature. Thus, the personal relationship with the personal Christ, for instance, is not symbolic. Precisely this existential attitude is constitutive for religion.

Bultmann said that Christianity is nothing other than existentialist philosophy. If a personal relationship, to the religion's founder, for instance, is important for a religion, it is at the same time more than an existential attitude. (KOSLOWSKI)

The significance of symbolism in religion can change. If the symbolism loses importance and becomes only marginal, the religion itself also changes. (IDEL)

The concrete form of religion is a combination of symbolism and existential-ism. (HORUZHY)

Max Scheler spoke of "salvation knowledge." This salvation knowledge is to be sure not actual knowledge, but it can help people to change and to improve existentially, which need not absolutely happen through philosophy. Philosophy does not have this element at its disposal, while, on the other hand, there is existentialist philosophy, which is no longer neutral.

2. Religion and Philosophy

In this Discourse of the World Religions, should the religions be considered from the perspective of philosophy? Is the idea that philosophy can build a bridge between the religions meaningful? Or would that overestimate philosophy? In Germany philosophy and religion are increasingly seen as opposing one another. Consequently, a philosopher who is interested in religion almost seems today not to be serious. (KOSLOWSKI)

In the Islamic tradition philosophy is distinguished from religion, since philosophy's sources are Greek and not Islamic. Thus, the most famous Islamic philosophers referred above all to Aristotle. (ENGINEER)

An historical comment regarding the problem of religion vs. philosophy: Sergei Bulgakov was the founder of a philosophical institute in Paris and converted to Christianity, because he saw that philosophy is in principle incapable of making true statements about dogmas and religion. In this sense, philosophy is always heretical. (HORUZHY)

In Russian thought there seems to be a tendency toward theosophy. That means that philosophy alone cannot give us what we need; but neither can theology, because – for modern man – it cannot simply put forward a dogma and thereby cause it to be believed. Since this is a problem, a connection between theology and philosophy must be found. (KOSLOWSKI)

Drawing a line between philosophy and religion is extremely difficult. Christianity obligates people to believe in dogmas; philosophy does not. (HORUZHY)

The role of dogma is a very important point for our discussion. Within Christianity there are confessional differences with respect to dogma. Protestants would not accept a dogma merely because it has been established. Dogma exists for them only because it is in Scripture. A dogma is valid for Catholics, first, because it is in Scripture, second, because it is part of Tradition, and third, because the Pope has established it as a dogma. Furthermore, the canon of the Holy Scriptures is not unambiguous. There is no principle according to which it can be decided which texts belong to it and which do not. How is that in the other religions? Who decides which propositions are important? (KOSLOWSKI)

Quite early in the history of Buddhism, three councils took place, the first presumably immediately after Buddha's death. The Sutras, Teachings, and Sermons of Buddha were read and discussed at these councils. (ANTARKAR)

That upon which the religions are based has not been handed down as dogma, but instead began as a revelation that was experienced. Therefore, we must ask what the revelation says. (D'SA)

Philosophy is a part of the process of self-understanding, because it attempts to clarify the principles that stand behind a dogma. In this attempt, however, it creates antagonisms and plays the role of an outsider. This is the status of philosophy in the religion of revelation. (IDEL)

Two types of philosophical attitude must be distinguished here. There is a philosophical attitude that defines itself as non-religious and assumes that it has a self-sufficient intellect or set of ideas. The other attitude relates itself directly toward religion and understands itself to be amplifying religion. (HORUZHY)

Philosophy can, in extreme cases, regard itself as an alternative to religion. (IDEL).

Thomas Aquinas took up Aristotle because he did not have a theological system of his own and was in this respect open. Thus Thomas could support his system with Aristotle. The late Schelling criticized this form. He said that it is obvious that the Church regarded Aristotelian philosophy merely as the handmaiden of theology. Is this relation to philosophy specifically Christian? (KOSLOWSKI)

There is yet another Christian understanding of philosophy: that of Heidegger. He said that philosophy made sense only for the Greeks. Therefore, there could be no such thing as Christian philosophy. This critique seems to be very close to Islam's critique of philosophy. (HORUZHY)

Islam's relationship to philosophy is different from that. The philosopher speaks the language of the intellectuals; the prophet the language of the masses. The subject matter is the same; only the function is different. The prophet leads the masses; the philosopher cannot do so. (ENGINEER)

In reply to a question about the Sanskrit word for "philosophy," RAMAN said that the equivalent can presumable be found in the term "anviksiki," which means "critical discussion with the faith."

3. Law and Cosmic Order

There appears to be a consensus that law is of great importance for the religions. How is the concept of law understood in the various religions? (KOSLOWSKI)

"Tora" means instructions for a possible path. Therefore, it is understood more as instructions for action and not only as a law. (IDEL)

Instructions, however, are institutions, like the law. Is that the common feature of the religions: Telling people how they should regulate their lives by institutions? (KOSLOWSKI)

The term "*dharma*," which is the word for religion, literally means "law." The law, which was brought into the world by an inspired person, is also used in Buddhist metaphysics in a very wide sense. It includes the moral law. Furthermore, the *Bhagavad-Gita* is concerned not only with the social order, but also with the cosmic order. God comes into the world through this law. (RAMAN)

There exists a difference here between Western and Eastern traditions. Revelation is especially interesting for Islam, Judaism, and Christianity, as original, non-cosmic order. Revelation here is the way to integrate human persons into a larger, cosmic order. (IDEL)

In Hinduism, "*rita*" is the natural order, from which the later concept of *dharma* originated. It went beyond the natural order and also included the moral order. In this sense, early Hinduism is pantheistic: Religious consciousness coincided with the natural order. (RAMAN)

Buddhism was a kind of protest religion against Hinduism. Protest against a social order must also include protest against the natural order. In the case of Catholicism, it was different. The Protestants rejected the idea of natural law, because the considered it not to be biblical. This raises the question whether religions are at all changeable. One could say that Christianity, as it was adopted by the Roman Empire, changed from a protest religion to an established religion. (KOSLOWSKI)

Buddhist historians agree that Buddhism was not a metaphysical protest against Hinduism, because many Hindu elements were taken over by Buddhist philosophy. Buddhism is a protest against the social order. (RAMAN)

In Hinduism, theistic and non-theistic elements are united in one and the same religion. But Buddhism does not belong to the six classical Indian systems. What distinguishes Buddhism as a non-theistic religion from, for example, the Sāṅkhya tradition? Why is atheistic Sāṅkhya part of Hindu orthodoxy and what does this imply? (Koslowski)

Belonging to Hinduism includes both the desire for community and acknowledgment of the vedic order. (ANTARKAR)

The question is not whether a system is theistic, but whether it accepts the Vedas. Here the understanding of Puruṣa, the primordial cosmic giant, the absolute person, from whom the cosmos originated, is of significance. The vedic understanding of Puruṣa is accepted in the Sāṅkhya tradition. By its dualistic interpretation of the primordial cosmic being, the cosmos is understood as a micro-macro-cosmos. (D'SA)

Perhaps the relationship between revelation and cosmic order can be explained more precisely. In the Western traditions, revelation is revelation of the divine will, which is distinguished from the world. In the Hindu and Buddhist systems, on the contrary, the will of God is much less important. In the biblical religions, God's wisdom originated from God's will, and the order of the world, which God connected to reality, originated from God's wisdom. In India this connection existed from the beginning and was not a result of later developments. (IDEL)

That is true, however, only of vedic religion. Only it begins with the cosmic order and is connected to the natural law. (ANTARKAR and RAMAN)

In the vedic texts there is no word for reality other than "cosmic hallowing." This hallowing, in which God as a natural force hollows itself, is the hub of the world, that which holds reality together. This meaning of "hallowing" is to be distinguished from that of Christianity and Judaism and means that everything lives from everything, for everything, and with everything. In connection with *dharma*, this means that life means repaying this debt. (D'SA)

4. Mythology

In Christianity and Judaism, mythology is what is supposed to have been left behind. Mythology is in this sense "false" religion. The demythologization of Christianity was the attempt to find the true religion. The Abrahamic religions polemicize in this respect against mythology. (KOSLOWSKI)

Mythology means, to begin with, only a set of different stories. Even so, some religions are quite mythologically oriented, without having such a set of narratives at their disposal. And there are other religions that cannot be called mythological, even though that possess a mythology. Therefore, having much mythology is insufficient to make a religion mythological. (IDEL)

Drawing a line here is difficult. Traditionally, mythology was polytheism, and therefore meant heathenism (or paganism). That is a polemical concept, but is advocated in the Abrahamic religions. Christianity has traditionally regarded Hinduism as pagan. It has a concept of God that is polytheistic and mythological. Is the proposition "Hinduism is a mythology" justified? (KOSLOWSKI)

In some forms of Hinduism, such as Vaishyaism or Vishnuism, which has no texts of its own, it would be accepted that it has something to do with mythology. In contrast, the "Viraisaivas," a social-reform sect of Shivaism, is the only sect of Hinduism that has many elements of a prophetic religion, e.g. texts that prescribe a strict social order. The metaphorical element appears indeed to be common to them, although in their entirety they are quite different. (RAMAN)

Buddhism also has a mythology with non-historical figures. (ANTARKAR)

CONTRIBUTORS

ERNST ALBRECHT, born 1930; B.A., Dr. rer. pol. Member of the Parliament of Lower Saxony, Hanover, Germany, 1970-90; Minister-President of Lower Saxony, 1976-90; Vice-Chairman of the Christian Democratic Union of Germany, 1979-90; Founder and President, Stiftung Niedersachsen – The Foundation of Lower Saxony, 1985-2000; Personal Advisor to the President and the Prime Minister of Kyrgyzstan, since 1995. Publications include: *Der Staat: Idee und Wirklichkeit* (Stuttgart, 1976); *Erinnerungen, Erkenntnisse, Entscheidungen* (Göttingen, 1999).

SHIVRAM S. ANTARKAR, born 1931, Maharashtra, India; M.A., Ph.D., Philosophy, University of Mumbai. Retired in 1991 as Professor and Head of the Department of Philosophy, University of Mumbai; currently, Honorary Professor, in charge of the Jain Academy Educational and Research Center, Department of Philosophy, University of Mumbai. Publications include: 25 articles in the *Marathi Encyclopaedia of Philosophy* (Pune, 1974); trans. into Marathi of A. J. Ayer, *Language, Truth and Logic* (Pune, 1974); *Religious Life and Scientific Outlook* (Pune, 1981).

MICHA BRUMLIK, born 1947, Davos, Switzerland; Dr. phil. Professor of Education, Heidelberg University, 1981-2000, Frankfurt University, 2000-present. Publications include: *Advokatorische Ethik: Zur Legitimation pädagogischer Eingriffe* (Bielefeld, 1992); *Die Gnostiker: Der Traum von der Selbsterlösung des Menschen* (Frankfurt, 1992); *C. G. Jung: Zur Einführung* (Hamburg, 1993); *Schrift, Wort und Ikone: Wege aus dem Bilderverbot* (Frankfurt, 1994); *Gerechtigkeit zwischen den Generationen* (Berlin, 1996); *Kein Weg als Deutscher und Jude: Eine bundesrepublikanische Erfahrung* (Munich, 1996); *Deutscher Geist und Judenhaß: Das Verhältnis des philosophischen Idealismus zum Judentum* (Munich, 2000); *Vernunft und Offenbarung: Religionsphilosophische Aufsätze* (Berlin, 2001).

D. P. CHATTOPADHYAYA, LL.B., M.A., Ph.D. (Calcutta and London School of Economics), D.Litt. h.c. Professor Emeritus, Jadavpur University, Calcutta; Founding Director, Indian Council of Philosophical Research; Former President, Indian Institute of Advanced Study; Director, Centre for Studies in Civilizations, Calcutta and Delhi. Publications include: *Interdisciplinary Studies in*

Science, Technology, Philosophy and Culture (New Delhi, 1996); *Science, Philosophy and Culture: Multi-Disciplinary Explorations* (New Delhi, 1996/97); *Sociology, Ideology and Utopia* (Leiden, 1997); Co-Editor, *Cultural Otherness and Beyond* (Leiden, 1998); *Societies, Cultures and Ideologies* (Mumbai, 2000); General Editor, *History of Science, Philosophy and Culture in Indian Civilization*, 50 vols. (New Delhi, 2000-).

FRANCIS X. D'SA, born 1936, Gokak Falls, Belgaum District, Karnataka State, India. Professor, Department of Systematic Theology and Indian Religions, Pontifical Athenaeum, Pune; Director, Institute for the Study of Religion, Pune, India. Publications include: *Shabdapramanyam in Shabara and Kumarila* (Vienna, 1980); Editor, *Word-Index to the Baghavadgita* (Pune, 1985); *Gott, der Dreieine und der All-Ganze* (Düsseldorf, 1987); Co-Editor, *Hermeneutics of Encounter* (Vienna, 1994); Editor, *The Dharma of Jesus* (Pune, 1997); Co-Author, *The World as Sacrament* (Pune, 1998).

ASHGAR ALI ENGINEER, born 1940 in India; Graduate in Civil Engineering; D.Lit.h.c., University of Calcutta, 1993. Studied Islamic Theology, Tafsir (Commentary on the Holy Qur'an), Islamic Jurisprudence, and Hadith; has lectured in many universities in the USA, Canada, Great Britain, Switzerland, Thailand, Malaysia, Indonesia, Sri Lanka, Pakistan, Yemen, Egypt, HongKong, etc. Publications include: *The Bohras* (New Delhi, 1980); *Islam and its Relevance to our Age* (Mumbai, 1984); *Islam and Muslims: Critical Perspectives* (Jaipur, 1985); *Communalism and Communal Violence in India* (Delhi, 1985); *Ethnic Conflicts in South Asia* (Delhi, 1987); *Rights of Women in Islam* (Delhi, 1992); *The Origin and Development of Islam* (Mumbai, 1992); and many other books (a total of forty-five).

FRIEDRICH HERMANNI, born 1958; Dr. Phil. Habil., Pastor. Research Fellow, Hanover Institute of Philosophical Research, 1993-2000. Publications include: *Die letzte Entlastung: Vollendung und Scheitern des abendländischen Theodizeeprojektes in Schellings Philosophie* (1994); Co-Editor, *Philosophische Orientierung* (1995); Co-Author, *Die Wirklichkeit des Bösen: Systematisch-theologische und philosophische Annäherungen* (1998); Co-Editor, *Der leidende Gott: Eine philosophische und theologische Kritik* (2001).

SERGEY S. HORUZHY, born 1941; Ph.D., Theoretical Physics, Moscow State University. Professor of Mathematical Physics, Mathematical Institute Steklov, Russian Academy of Science. Publications include: (in Russian) *Introduction to Algebraic Quantum Field Theory* (Moscow, 1986); *Diptych of Silence: Ascetic Anthropology in Theological and Philosophical Presentation* (Moscow, 1991); *After the Interruption: Ways of Russian Philosophy* (St. Petersburg, 1994);

"Ulysses" in a Russian Mirror (Moscow, 1994); *Synergy: Problems of Orthodox Asceticism and Mysticism* (Moscow, 1995); *On the Phenomenology of Ascesis* (Moscow, 1998); *The World View of Pavel Florensky* (Tomsk, 1999); (in English) *Philosophy and Ascesis* (Lewiston, N. Y., 1999).

MOSHE IDEL, Professor of Jewish Studies, Hebrew University Jerusalem. (For more details, see A Discourse of the World Religions, Vol. 4.)

PETER KOSLOWSKI, born 1952, Göttingen, Germany. Independent Author; Adjunct Professor of Philosophy and Political Economy, University of Witten/ Herdecke; Founding Director, Forschungsinstitut für Philosophie Hannover – The Hanover Institute of Philosophical Research, 1987-2001. Publications include: *Gesellschaft und Staat: Ein unvermeidlicher Dualismus* (Stuttgart, 1982; Russian edition); *Die postmoderne Kultur* (Munich, 1987, 1988; Chinese, Italian, Japanese, Russian editions); Series Editor, *Studies in Economic Ethics and Philosophy*, 30 vols. (Heidelberg and New York, since 1992); *Gnosis und Theodizee* (Vienna, 1993); Editor, *Die spekulative Philosophie der Weltreligionen* (Vienna, 1997); Co-Editor, *Die Wirklichkeit des Bösen* (Munich, 1998); *Principles of Ethical Economy* (Dordrecht, 2001; Chinese, French, German, Russian, Spanish editions); *Philosophien der Offenbarung: Antiker Gnostizismus, Franz von Baader* (Paderborn, 2001).

N. S. S. RAMAN, Professor Emeritus of Philosophy and Religion, Banaras Hindu University, Varanasi, India. (For details, see A Discourse of the World Religions, Vol. 4.)

MUHAMMAD SHAMA, Professor and Head of the Department of Islamic Studies, al-Azhar University, Cairo. (For details, see A Discourse of the World Religions, Vol. 4.)

INDEX OF PERSONS

Italicized page numbers refer to names in footnotes.

Peter Koslowski, Editor

The Concept of God, the Origin of the World, and the Image of the Human in the World Religions

A Discourse of the World Religions 1

All religions make statements about God or the Absolute and about "the beginning": about the beginning of the world and the beginning and nature of the human person. Propositions about God, the human person, and the world, statements about God's eternity or process of becoming, about the status and nature of the human person as the "image of God," and about the beginning of the world are woven into "religious speculations about the beginning." The theology, anthropology, and cosmology of the world religions determine the image of the human person and the image of the world in the world cultures shaped by the different religions. They stand in a tense relationship with the anthropologies and cosmologies of modern science, which in turn challenge the religions to deepen their image of the human person.

The first of the five volumes in the series A Discourse of the World Religions presents the image of the human person and the image of the deity in the world religions, as well as their teachings about the beginning of the world. With their contributions to this volume – and to the other four volumes in the series – leading scholars of Hinduism, Buddhism, Judaism, Christianity, and Islam have produced a first-hand source of information, which enables the reader to understand better the five world religions and their central teachings.

Contents:

Peter Koslowski, Editor
The Origin and the Overcoming of Evil and Suffering in the World Religions
A Discourse of the World Religions 2

All religions face the challenge of explaining, in view of God's goodness, the existence of evil and suffering in the world. They must develop theories of the origin and the overcoming of evil and suffering. The explanations of evil and suffering in the various religions, as well as their theories of the origin and the overcoming of evil and suffering, differ from one another, but are also similar in many respects. The human person is always considered to be the origin of evil, and also to be the focus of aspirations to be able to overcome evil. The conviction that evil and suffering are not original and can be overcome is shared by and is essential to the world religions.

The explanations of the origin of evil are related to the explanations of the continuation and propagation of evil in human persons, in nature, and in our technology and culture that have been developed in the religions – in Christianity, for example, as the doctrine of original sin. Finally, the world religions are concerned with how to cope with suffering and offer guidance for overcoming it.

Contents:

Peter Koslowski, Editor

The Progress and End of History, Life after Death, and Resurrection of the Human Person in the World Religions
A Discourse of the World Religions 4

The fourth volume in the series examines the interpretation of history in the religions. The world religions offer more than an interpretation of present history and the present world and existence of the human race. They also convey to humankind a theory of world history and of history before and above world history. Part of the interpretation of history in the religions may be a conception of the apocalypse or the eschatological revelation of transcendent reality and the eschatological transformation and completion of this world.

The propositions of the world religions concerning the end of history and the revelation of the completion of the world are related to the question of the completion of the individual human life and human immortality. Immortality is described in the Abrahamic religions as personal resurrection; in Hinduism as entering the divine self, the Ātman; and in Buddhism as being united with the Buddha. How do the religions interpret universal history and what statements to they make about life after death?

Contents:

Peter Koslowski, Editor
Philosophical Dialogue of the Religions instead of the Clash of Civilizations in the Process of Globalization
A Discourse of the World Religions 5

Religions are the largest communities of the global society and claim, at least in the cases of Islam and Christianity, to be universal interpretations of life and orders of existence. With the globalization of the world economy and the unity of the global society in the "Internet," they gain unprecedented access to the entire human race through modern means of communication. At the same time, this globalization brings religions into conflict with one another in their claims to universal validity. How can the conflict of religions be defused? The speculative, philosophical method of dealing with a religion is a way to present one's own religious convictions in the medium of philosophy and rational discourse. The philosophical approach to religion can serve as the basis of the conversation of the world religions, without dissolving their truth claims. It can reduce dogmatic claims and contribute to overcoming fundamentalism. Philosophy builds bridges between religions.

Contents: